The Wedding Planner

GOBLE & SHEA'S COMPLETE

Wedding Planner

Kathleen Goble & Cecily Shea

Multnomah Publisher's, Inc. Sisters, Oregon

GOBLE & SHEA'S COMPLETE WEDDING PLANNER
published by Multnomah Publishers, Inc.

Copyright ©1999 by Kathleen Goble and Cecily Shea
International Standard Book Number: 1-57673-481-1

The first edition of this book was printed in 1989
with ISBN 0-945564-10-4

Cover photograph by Andrea Gjeldum
Design by Andrea Gjeldum

Multnomah is a trademark of Multnomah Publishers, Inc.,
and is registered in the U.S. Patent and Trademark Office.
The colophon is a trademark of Multnomah Publishers, Inc.

Printed in the United States of America

For information:
MULTNOMAH PUBLISHERS, INC.
POST OFFICE BOX 1720
SISTERS, OREGON 97759

           Library of Congress Cataloging-in-Publication Data

Goble, Kathleen.
    Goble & Shea's complete wedding planner : for the organized and
relaxed bride / Kathleen Goble & Cecily Shea.
        p.   cm.
    ISBN 1-57673-481-1 (alk. paper)
    1. Weddings--Planning. 2. Wedding etiquette.   I. Shea, Cecily.
II. Title. III. Title: Complete wedding planner.   IV. Title: Goble
and Shea's complete wedding planner.
    HQ745.G6   1999
    395.2'2--dc21

99 00 01 02 03 04 05 — 18 17 16 15 14 13

THIS BOOK
IS A TREASURE AND A KEEPSAKE,
A FAMILY HEIRLOOM IN THE MAKING
TO BE CHERISHED FOREVER...
AND IT BELONGS TO

_____

CONTENTS

OUR ENGAGEMENT KEEPSAKE

My fiancé's name _____ Where he lives _____

His parents names _____ Where they live _____

Where we were when he asked me to marry him _____

What he said to me _____

What I said to him _____

What I was wearing _____

What he was wearing _____

What we were doing _____

_____

How we told my parents _____

What we said _____

_____

What they said _____

_____

How we told his parents _____

_____

What we said _____

_____

What they said _____

_____

How we told our friends _____

_____

Additional keepsakes _____

_____

PREFACE

While planning the weddings of Cecily and her brother Jeff—two weddings in thirteen days!—we became inundated by the myriad details involved in pulling off the events successfully. We knew the only way to survive and to really enjoy the weddings (which we were determined to do!) would be to keep organized.

When we consulted wedding books, the suggested organizational tools, although worthwhile, were all in addition to having a book to guide us. Before long, the tools themselves became part of the clutter as the wedding apparel, trousseau, gifts, and decorations began to fill the house. Things were misplaced, causing wasted time and frazzled nerves in the effort to put our hands on the exact information we were seeking.

Through it all, the idea was born to have everything in one location, using only one tool—an organizational planner for weddings. Building upon the experience we gained while planning our family's weddings, we added countless hours of research during the writing of the book. This updated version has been fine-tuned even more as a result of more years spent coordinating weddings.

Since the first printing of Goble & Shea's Complete Wedding Planner, we have received glowing endorsements from brides throughout the United States and Canada. Many of these brides—some of whom were actively pursuing careers—found our book to be an invaluable resource. One of the most remarkable testimonials we heard was from a woman who had only two weeks to prepare for her wedding, between the time she finished her finals in medical school and the start of her hospital internship. She wrote, "I couldn't have done it without your book."

So regardless of the amount of time you have to plan your wedding, this book can help you organize your time, plan the essentials, carry out the details, and "get you to the church on time."

INTRODUCTION

In recent years we've seen a resurgence in the popularity of the traditional wedding style. Most couples, however, are not holding to the rigid structure of the past but are incorporating the best of the contemporary styles to reflect their own lifestyles and personalities.

Like every bride, you have a familiarity with weddings and an idea of what you want your own to be like. But how do you translate your knowledge of weddings into a workable plan? How do you utilize your time effectively? These are the key questions this book addresses while guiding you in planning the wedding of your dreams.

There is more to planning a wedding than collecting something old, something new, something borrowed, and something blue—although this wedding tradition could be a bride's first step in organization. This book is a complete resource for planning your wedding; and by using this book, you and your fiancée will succeed in accomplishing each detail. In order to utilize this book most effectively, we suggest the following steps:

- Take a few minutes to familiarize yourself with the material in the book.
- Read the Planning Checklist and make note of the items that are appropriate for your wedding. Then incorporate these items into the Calendar.
- Use only the worksheets and lists you find helpful.

Planning a wedding is often the first opportunity a bridal couple have to work together on a project. It offers an invaluable learning experience, one that will help in the adjustment process once you are married. You may enlist family members and friends to help in the planning process. People usually feel honored when asked for assistance. For those who may be low on funds, it offers them an opportunity to give a gift of time and service.

Above all, remember not to allow the wedding details to overshadow you and your fiancé's relationship. Nurturing this relationship now is vitally important to your future happiness. We highly recommend that you, as a couple, either participate in premarital counseling or attend a marriage preparation class (many churches, synagogues, and family counseling centers provide these services). No one wants to think their marriage will end in divorce, and by preparing in this way, you will lessen the probability of it happening to you.

If you feel divorce can be a "way out," then maybe you are not ready for marriage. More than anything else, a high level of commitment is the necessary ingredient in a successful marriage—and that commitment is to endure the bad times as well as the good.

Remember to set aside time before the wedding to become better acquainted with the parents of the one you love; without them, this wouldn't be happening!

Finally, don't take yourself or the planning too seriously. Instead, take plenty of time to relax, to enjoy each other, and to grow in love!

Planning Checklists

Planning Checklists
How-To

- After you've had the chance to familiarize yourself with the entire book, read through the Planning Checklists and make a note of the items that are appropriate to your situation. Then incorporate those items into your planning calendars (which begin on page 15).

- Some weddings are planned in fewer than six months. This checklist can be tailored to fit your particular time frame.

- Today's grooms are taking a more active role in planning their weddings. So provide your fiancé with a copy of the Groom's Planning Checklist. Having this list will help eliminate any confusion he may feel about the wedding planning process. And by knowing what needs to be done, he'll be able to participate as fully as he desires.

BRIDE'S PLANNING CHECKLIST

Six to Twelve Months Before

❑ Incorporate items from this Planning Checklist into your Complete Wedding Planner calendar (beginning on page 15).

❑ Set a budget for the wedding, working together with those responsible. Use the information on estimated cost percentages on page 38. Record the agreed amounts on Worksheet 1 (pages 41–42).

❑ Complete Worksheet 3 (page 49) with your fiancé to record your choices for the style (degree of formality) of your wedding; the wedding date and time; and the wedding location.

❑ Select and reserve your ceremony site using Worksheet 5 (page 51). You should also reserve a time now for the wedding rehearsal.

❑ Select and reserve your reception site using Worksheets 14 and 15 (pages 120–21).

❑ Coordinate the date and time you've chosen with both the ceremony and reception sites.

❑ Use Worksheet 4 (page 50) as you select the officiant for the wedding ceremony.

❑ If you decide to consult with a wedding coordinator, use Worksheet 8 (page 65) as you meet with various candidates and decide which one to use.

❑ Confirm the wedding and rehearsal times and dates with your officiant and/or wedding coordinator.

❑ Arrange for premarital counseling or marriage preparation classes with your officiant or a family counseling center.

❑ Decide on the approximate number of guests and begin to compile a tentative list.

❑ Select the color scheme for your wedding and reception.

❑ Use the Wedding Gown Search List (page 80) and Worksheet 9 (page 81) as you shop for your wedding gown, headpiece, veil, and other accessories.

❑ Soon after setting a wedding date, select your attendants and invite them to participate.

❑ Use the Bridal Attendants List (page 92) to record their names, addresses, phone numbers, and clothing sizes.

❑ Select and order your bridal attendants' dresses. Use Worksheet 11 (page 91) to help in this process.

❑ Talk with the mothers about their dresses for the wedding.

❑ Use the worksheets indicated below as you select professionals to provide the following for your special day...

    ❑ music (Worksheet 25, page 148)

    ❑ flowers (Worksheet 28, page 157)

    ❑ photography (Worksheet 30, page 166)

    ❑ reception catering (Worksheet 16, page 122)

    ❑ cake (Worksheet 19, page 125)

    ❑ videotaping and audiotaping (Worksheet 31 and 33, pages 169 and 171)

These professionals often are booked months in advance, so contact them as early as possible.

❑ Register with the bridal gift registry of your favorite store. Use the Gift Registry (pages 234–43) as a guide to your selection of possible gift choices.

Three to Six Months Before

❑ Set a deadline no later than three months before the wedding date for your families' completed guest lists.

❑ Use Worksheets 22 and 23 (pages 141–43) as you order the invitations, announcements, enclosures, and other personal stationery and accessories.

❑ Order your groom's ring.

❑ Coordinate the rehearsal dinner with the groom's parents.

❑ Provide the rehearsal dinner hosts with a list of guests to be invited (use the form on pages 206–7).

❑ Use the guest lists on pages 195–7 when compiling names for bridal shower hostesses.

❑ Continue using Worksheet 9 (page 81) as you shop for wedding attire and accessories.

❑ Tell each bridal attendant where their bridal accessories may be purchased.

❑ Coordinate your wardrobe with the trousseau inventory in Worksheet 10 (page 83).

Schedule appointments for your...

❑ physical examination   ❑ dental examination   ❑ eye examination

❑ Begin looking for a place to live. If you plan to rent, consult the Rental Housing Checklist (pages 224–5).

❑ Use the Home Furnishings Purchase Plan (page 228) and Worksheet 51 (Keep or Toss, page 230) as you plan and shop for home furnishings.

❑ Discuss honeymoon plans with your fiancé.

Two Months Before

❑ As gifts arrive, enter descriptions into the gift record of the Guest List section, and write thank-you notes. If local custom or family tradition warrants, plan a gift display area in your home.

❑ Address and mail invitations four to six weeks before the wedding.

❑ Buy and wrap your groom's wedding gift.

❑ Buy and wrap your bridal attendants' gifts. Note these gifts on the Bridal Attendants List on page 92.

❑ Check on the delivery dates of your gown and the attendants' dresses.

❑ As you decide on the clothes for your honeymoon, use the checklist on page 84.

❑ Plan where to dress on your wedding day.

❑ Schedule formal bridal portrait.

❑ Schedule fittings for your gown.

❑ Schedule an appointment with your hairstylist to design your hairstyle for the wedding day.

❑ As you and your fiancé meet with the officiant to plan the order of your wedding ceremony, use Worksheets 6 and 7 (pages 60–61).

❑ Plan your wedding music. To help you, use the list of musical selection ideas on page 147, plus the worksheets and guidelines on pages 148–53.

❑ Finalize plans with the florist. Use the worksheets and other guides on pages 157–63.

❑ Finalize plans with the photographer. Use Worksheet 30 (page 166) and the planning list and guidelines on page 167.

❑ Finalize reception plans with the caterer. Use Worksheets 17 and 18 (pages 123–24), plus the diagrams on page 129.

❑ Finalize plans for the wedding cake with the bakery, using Worksheet 20 (page 126).

❑ Use Worksheet 32 (page 170) to finalize plans for videotaping.

❑ Use Worksheet 34 (page 172) to finalize plans for audiotaping.

❑ Plan the wedding rehearsal with the officiant and/or wedding coordinator. Use the Rehearsal Information List on pages 72–73.

- ❑ Use Worksheet 35 (page 175) as you make lodging or travel plans for out-of-town guests.
- ❑ To arrange for wedding day transportation for the wedding party, use Worksheets 36 and 37 (pages 178–79).
- ❑ Order any rental equipment needed for the wedding and reception. Refer to the Equipment List on pages 181–86 for any accessory ideas.

One Month Before

- ❑ Have your groom's ring engraved.
- ❑ Continue writing thank-you notes as gifts arrive.
- ❑ Address your wedding announcements.
- ❑ Make arrangements for the bridal luncheon (or dinner or party) for your bridal attendants. Use the guest list and worksheets on pages 198–200.
- ❑ Write or phone invitations to your attendants for the bridal luncheon.
- ❑ Confirm that your attendants have purchased their wedding accessories.
- ❑ If the attendants' shoes are being dyed to match, have them done at this time.
- ❑ Have each bridal attendant be responsible for making and keeping her own fittings.
- ❑ Schedule an appointment to have your nails done a day or two before the wedding.
- ❑ Schedule an appointment to have your hair and makeup done on the wedding day.
- ❑ Start packing your personal belongings for moving.
- ❑ Make plans for the preceremony buffet on the wedding day. Use the guest list and worksheet on pages 201–2.
- ❑ Make any necessary arrangements for after-the-wedding cleanup, return of rental equipment, and transportation of gifts. For assistance, use the Reception Organizer on pages 130–31 and Worksheet 38 on page 187.
- ❑ Discuss future financial details with your fiancé.
- ❑ Refer to the Financial/Legal Checklist on page 222 for any needed name, address, or beneficiary changes.
- ❑ Use Worksheet 48 (page 218) as you check on your state's marriage requirements.
- ❑ If necessary, have premarital blood tests taken.
- ❑ Go with your fiancé to obtain your marriage license.

Two Weeks Before

❏ Continue writing thank-you notes.

❏ Begin keeping your wedding day clothes in one place. Check them off, using the Bride's Wedding Day Checklist on page 85.

❏ Pack your clothes for the honeymoon, using the checklist on page 84.

❏ Give a copy of the Bridal Attendants' Guidelines (page 93) to each attendant.

❏ Use Worksheet 49 (page 220) as a guide for writing your wedding announcement for the newspaper, and prepare to have it delivered to the society editor.

❏ Have the ceremony programs printed.

❏ Obtain a floater insurance policy, if necessary, to cover your wedding gifts until you obtain a homeowner's or renter's policy.

❏ Arrange for someone to be at your home on the wedding day to answer the phone and keep an eye on things while the family is away.

❏ Make arrangements, if necessary, for a policeman or other attendant to direct traffic and parking for the ceremony and reception.

❏ Arrange for someone to mail your wedding announcements immediately after the wedding.

❏ Send final information on guest housing and transportation (see page 176) to your out-of-town guests.

❏ Give the list of Transportation Guidelines for Drivers (page 177) to those who will be driving out-of-town guests.

One Week Before

❏ Keep writing those thank-you notes.

❏ Have a final fitting for your wedding gown.

❏ Find something to protect your gown—tissue paper, plastic, or a sheet—while transporting it to the ceremony site.

Make arrangements for delivery or pickup of...

❏ dresses   ❏ beverages

❏ wedding cake   ❏ rental equipment, etc.

Double-check all plans with phone calls to these people:

- ❏ coordinator for ceremony site
- ❏ officiant
- ❏ musicians
- ❏ florist
- ❏ photographer
- ❏ video operator
- ❏ audio operator
- ❏ coordinator for reception site
- ❏ caterer
- ❏ cake baker
- ❏ provider of rental equipment
- ❏ provider of limo service

❏ Check on outdoor automatic lighting and watering schedules for any time conflict with the ceremony or reception.

❏ If necessary, make any phone calls to late respondents for the reception head count.

❏ Confirm the number of acceptances with the reception site and caterer.

❏ Prepare seating charts or place cards for the reception.

❏ Make up an emergency kit—needle, thread, safety pins, bobby pins, tissues, etc.—to be taken to the ceremony site.

❏ If any festivities are to be held at your home, arrange to board your pets for the day.

❏ Attend your bridal luncheon with your attendants.

One Day Before

❏ Complete all decorating (have bridal attendants help).

❏ Have your nails done.

❏ Attend the rehearsal.

❏ Give a copy of Worksheet 13 (Ushers' Assignments, page 106) to the head usher at the rehearsal.

❏ Attend the rehearsal dinner.

Your Wedding Day

❏ Eat light meals, avoiding spicy and fried foods.

❏ Enjoy a relaxing bath.

❏ Finish packing for your honeymoon.

❏ Have your hair styled and makeup applied.

❏ Dress for the wedding.

❏ Enjoy your day!

GROOM'S PLANNING
CHECKLIST

Six to Twelve Months Before

❑ Determine the wedding budget with your fiancée and your families. Use Worksheet 2 (pages 43–44) as a checklist for your financial responsibilities.

❑ Discuss ceremony and reception sites with your fiancée.

❑ Begin compiling a guest list with your family.

❑ With your fiancée, visit the officiant who will perform the ceremony.

❑ With your fiancée, take part in premarital counseling or marriage preparation classes.

❑ Select your best man and other attendants and invite them to participate. Write their names and addresses on the Groom's Attendants' List (pages 103–4).

❑ With your fiancée, discuss preferences for the Gift Registry (pages 234–43).

Three to Six Months Before

❑ Purchase your fiancée's engagement and wedding rings.

❑ Complete your guest list and give it to your fiancée no later than three months prior to the wedding.

❑ Decide on the style and color of your wedding attire and accessories (see Worksheet 12, page 94), and order as necessary.

❑ With your family, arrange for the rehearsal dinner. To assist you, use Worksheets 45–47 (pages 208–10) and the guest list on pages 206–7.

❑ With your fiancée, begin your search for your new home (see the checklist on pages 224–5).

❑ Plan and purchase needed home furnishings (see the checklists on pages 228–9).

❑ Discuss honeymoon plans with your fiancée, and use Worksheet 39 (pages 189–90) to begin making arrangements.

❑ If you plan to travel abroad, update passports, visas, and inoculations.

Schedule appointments for your...

❑ physical examination   ❑ dental examination   ❑ eye examination

❑ Decide on the attire for the fathers and your attendants, again using Worksheet 12 on page 94.

Two Months Before

❑ Plan the order of the wedding ceremony with your fiancée and the officiant.

❑ Purchase and wrap your gift for your fiancée.

❑ Purchase and wrap your gifts for your attendants.

❑ With your fiancée, make necessary housing and transportation arrangements for out-of-town guests.

❑ Complete your honeymoon plans, and make reservations.

❑ As needed, use Worksheet 50 (page 226) to plan your move into your new home.

One Month Before

❑ Have your fiancée's wedding ring engraved.

❑ Shop for any wedding or honeymoon attire you need.

❑ Confirm that your best man, ushers, and both fathers have ordered their wedding attire and have scheduled their fittings.

❑ If necessary for the marriage license, have premarital blood tests taken.

❑ Go with your fiancée to obtain your marriage license.

❑ Finalize plans for the rehearsal dinner.

❑ Address and mail—or phone—invitations to the Rehearsal Dinner.

❑ If you're having a bachelor party, make arrangements for it—using the guest list and Worksheets 43 and 44 on pages 204–5.

❑ Discuss future financial details with your fiancée, using the checklist on page 222.

Two Weeks Before

❑ Give copies of the Groom's Attendants' Guidelines (page 105) to the best man and ushers.

❑ Finalize plans for the bachelor party.

❑ Confirm all honeymoon arrangements.

❑ Begin packing to move.

One Week Before

❑ Schedule a haircut early in the week.

❑ Have a final fitting for your formal wear.

❑ Arrange for your transportation to the ceremony site.

- [ ] Confirm with your banquet manager the head count for the rehearsal dinner.
- [ ] Confirm with your banquet manager the head count for the bachelor party.
- [ ] Using the checklist on page 95, begin packing for the honeymoon.
- [ ] At the bachelor party or the rehearsal dinner, give gifts to your attendants.

One Day Before

- [ ] Pick up wedding attire.
- [ ] Use the checklist on page 96 to set aside clothes for the wedding and afterward.
- [ ] Attend the rehearsal.
- [ ] Attend the rehearsal dinner.

Your Wedding Day

- [ ] Eat light meals, avoiding spicy and fried foods.
- [ ] Enjoy a relaxing bath.
- [ ] Finish packing for your honeymoon.
- [ ] Give the wedding ring, marriage license, and envelope for the officiant to the best man.
- [ ] Designate someone to take care of any last-minute details.
- [ ] Dress for the wedding.
- [ ] Enjoy your day!

Calendars

CALENDARS HOW-TO

- Incorporate the appropriate items from your Planning Checklists (pages 3–11) into these calendars.

- Use the monthly calendars early in your planning, when there are fewer details to record. (Nine monthly calendars have been provided for you here.)

- As your list of things to do and remember grows longer during the last weeks before the wedding, you can keep track of them better by switching to the weekly calendars (twelve are provided here).

Saturday				
Friday				
Thursday				
Wednesday				
Tuesday				
Monday				
Sunday				

This Month

MONTHS TO GO

Saturday					
Friday					
Thursday					
Wednesday					
Tuesday					
Monday					
Sunday					

16

This Month

MONTHS TO GO

Saturday				
Friday				
Thursday				
Wednesday				
Tuesday				
Monday				
Sunday				

This Month

MONTHS TO GO

Saturday					
Friday					
Thursday					
Wednesday					
Tuesday					
Monday					
Sunday					

This Month

MONTHS TO GO

Saturday					
Friday					
Thursday					
Wednesday					
Tuesday					
Monday					
Sunday					

This Month

MONTHS TO GO

Saturday					
Friday					
Thursday					
Wednesday					
Tuesday					
Monday					
Sunday					

This Month

MONTHS TO GO

Saturday				
Friday				
Thursday				
Wednesday				
Tuesday				
Monday				
Sunday				

This Month

Saturday				
Friday				
Thursday				
Wednesday				
Tuesday				
Monday				
Sunday				

This Month

MONTHS TO GO

Saturday				
Friday				
Thursday				
Wednesday				
Tuesday				
Monday				
Sunday				

	MONDAY
Date	

	TUESDAY
Date	

	WEDNESDAY
Date	

	THURSDAY
Date	

	FRIDAY
Date	

	SATURDAY
Date	

	SUNDAY
Date	

	MONDAY
Date	

	TUESDAY
Date	

	WEDNESDAY
Date	

	THURSDAY
Date	

	FRIDAY
Date	

	SATURDAY
Date	

	SUNDAY
Date	

MONDAY

Date

TUESDAY

Date

WEDNESDAY

Date

THURSDAY

Date

FRIDAY

Date

SATURDAY

Date

SUNDAY

Date

	MONDAY
DATE	

	TUESDAY
DATE	

	WEDNESDAY
DATE	

	THURSDAY
DATE	

	FRIDAY
DATE	

	SATURDAY
DATE	

	SUNDAY
DATE	

MONDAY

Date

TUESDAY

Date

WEDNESDAY

Date

THURSDAY

Date

FRIDAY

Date

SATURDAY

Date

SUNDAY

Date

	MONDAY
DATE	

	TUESDAY
DATE	

	WEDNESDAY
DATE	

	THURSDAY
DATE	

	FRIDAY
DATE	

	SATURDAY
DATE	

	SUNDAY
DATE	

	MONDAY
Date	

	TUESDAY
Date	

	WEDNESDAY
Date	

	THURSDAY
Date	

	FRIDAY
Date	

	SATURDAY
Date	

	SUNDAY
Date	

Date	MONDAY

Date	TUESDAY

Date	WEDNESDAY

Date	THURSDAY

Date	FRIDAY

Date	SATURDAY

Date	SUNDAY

MONDAY

Date

TUESDAY

Date

WEDNESDAY

Date

THURSDAY

Date

FRIDAY

Date

SATURDAY

Date

SUNDAY

Date

Date	MONDAY

Date	TUESDAY

Date	WEDNESDAY

Date	THURSDAY

Date	FRIDAY

Date	SATURDAY

Date	SUNDAY

	MONDAY
DATE	

	TUESDAY
DATE	

	WEDNESDAY
DATE	

	THURSDAY
DATE	

	FRIDAY
DATE	

	SATURDAY
DATE	

	SUNDAY
DATE	

MONDAY

Date

TUESDAY

Date

WEDNESDAY

Date

THURSDAY

Date

FRIDAY

Date

SATURDAY

Date

SUNDAY

Date

Budget

BUDGET HOW-TO

- When forming your budget, decide first how much to spend for the wedding, then how the expenses will be divided.

- Paying for wedding expenses can be handled in a variety of ways. The responsibility can be
    - (a) assumed primarily by the bride's parents,
    - (b) assumed primarily by the groom's parents,
    - (c) shared equally by both sets of parents,
    - (d) shared by both families together with the bride and groom, or
    - (e) assumed entirely by the bride and groom themselves.

- Final responsibility for wedding costs has been stated by tradition, but there is really no right or wrong way to handle the costs. It's a matter of choice.

- It's appropriate to discuss the budget with both sets of parents, especially when they bear some or all of the financial responsibility. Be sure everyone involved agrees on the budget.

- A spirit of compromise should lessen the possibility of hurt feelings as your families agree together on the budget.

- When setting your budget priorities, compromise on quantity, not quality.

- The amount of your budget will not necessarily determine the style of your wedding; you can have a formal wedding and reception on a limited budget with careful planning and a smaller guest list.

- The following percentage estimates may be useful in breaking down your total wedding budget into categories:

stationery 4%	photography 9%
bridal attire 13%	bridesmaids' gifts 2%
music 4%	rentals 3%
reception 50%	transportation 2%
flowers 10%	miscellaneous fees 3%

- These percentages are a starting point for developing your budget and can be used as a tool when negotiating with various wedding services.

- To determine a guideline figure for each category in your budget, use this equation:

$$\text{your total budget} \quad x \quad \text{each item's estimated percentage}$$
$$\text{(from the list above)}$$

Example:

Assume that your total budget is $10,000, and you want to know a guideline for determining how much to spend for invitations and other stationery. Using the formula above, you multiply $10,000 times .04 (which is 4%, the estimate given above for stationery):

$$\$10,000 \quad x \quad .04 \quad = \quad \$400$$

Therefore, as a guideline for a $10,000 wedding budget, $400 would be an appropriate amount to spend on invitations and other stationery.

- You can change the percentages given above, depending on what you want to emphasize in your wedding.

- Prioritize the following aspects of a wedding according to what is most important to you:

  —number of guests to be invited

  —wedding site (church, synagogue, hotel, club, at home)

  —reception location (church hall, hotel, club, at home)

  —bridal attire (what you will wear)

  —food and beverages (what kind, and how will they be served)

  —flowers (what kind and how many)

  —photographs (to have a professional photographer or a friend take pictures)

  —music (soloists, live music or taped, dancing or not)

  —transportation (a limousine, luxury rental car, friend's new car, or family car)

- After having computed the amounts for each category, you may want to reevaluate your priorities. Make whatever adjustments are necessary to more closely meet your expectations.

- Once you've determined the amounts for each category, enter these amounts in the Amount Budgeted column on Worksheet I (Bride's Budget).

- For some expenses that are traditionally the groom's responsibility—such as certain flowers and his wedding attire—the cost will be determined by the overall wedding style. Other items in his budget will reflect his own preferences.

- Your budget should be flexible enough so that unexpected costs will not ruin it.

- You can usually expect to pay from 10 to 50 percent as a deposit for services. This deposit often is required in cash.

- You may want to consider opening a new checking account allotted for your wedding and reception expenses.

- Together you and your fiancé can use Worksheets I (Bride's Budget) and 2 (Groom's Budget) to keep a close tab on the budgeted amounts, total costs, deposits made, and the balance due in each category.

Worksheet 1

BRIDE'S BUDGET

(Traditional Expenses)

Budgeted Items	Amount Budgeted	Total Cost	Deposit	Balance Due
STATIONERY				
Invitations				
Reception cards				
Response cards				
Thank-you notes				
Napkins				
Matches				
Programs				
Announcements				
Postage				
BRIDAL ATTIRE	200			
Dress				
Headpiece and veil				
Accessories				
Bridal garter				
FAMILY ATTIRE				
Mother				
Father				
Sisters				
Brothers				
GROOM'S WEDDING RING AND GIFT	300			
BRIDAL ATTENDANTS' GIFTS				
BRIDE'S MEDICAL				
RECEPTION				
Site fee				
Caterer				
Food				
Beverages				
Gratuity and tax				
Cake				
Additional services				
MUSIC				
Ceremony				
Reception				

Budgeted Items	Amount Budgeted	Total Cost	Deposit	Balance Due
Florist	_____	_____		
Ceremony site flowers		_____	_____	_____
Bridesmaids' bouquets		_____	_____	_____
Groom's boutonniere		_____	_____	_____
Fathers' boutonnieres		_____	_____	_____
Reception site flowers		_____	_____	_____
Special others		_____	_____	_____
Candles		_____	_____	_____
Aisle runner		_____	_____	_____
Other		_____	_____	_____
Photographer	550	_____		
Formal portraits		_____	_____	_____
Engagement		_____	_____	_____
Wedding		_____	_____	_____
Wedding package		_____	_____	_____
Parents' albums		_____	_____	_____
Extra pictures		_____	_____	_____
Videotaping	0	_____	_____	_____
Audiotaping	0	_____	_____	_____
Special Parties	_____	_____		
Bridal luncheon		_____	_____	_____
Preceremony buffet		_____	_____	_____
Rental Equipment	_____	_____		
Ceremony		_____	_____	_____
Reception		_____	_____	_____
Transportation	_____	_____		
Parking attendant		_____	_____	_____
Car rental		_____	_____	_____
Miscellaneous Fees	_____	_____		
Ceremony site fee		_____	_____	_____
Wedding coordinator		_____	_____	_____
Maid service		_____	_____	_____
Guard for home		_____	_____	_____
Temporary insurance policy		_____	_____	_____
Unity candle		_____	_____	_____
Guest book		_____	_____	_____
Ring bearer's pillow		_____	_____	_____
Other		_____	_____	_____

GROOM'S BUDGET

(Traditional Expenses)

BUDGETED ITEMS	AMOUNT BUDGETED	TOTAL COST	DEPOSIT	BALANCE DUE
WEDDING ATTIRE	70			
Groom				
Mother				
Father				
Other				
HOUSING/TRANSPORTATION				
RINGS	100			
Engagement				
Wedding				
GIFT FOR THE BRIDE				
ATTENDANTS' GIFTS	60			
GROOM'S MEDICAL				
FLOWERS				
Bride's bouquet and corsage				
Mothers' corsages				
Grandmothers' corsages				
Ushers' boutonnieres				
BACHELOR PARTY				
REHEARSAL DINNER				
HONEYMOON EXPENSES				

(include an additional 10 percent to cover unexpected expenses)

MARRIAGE LICENSE	30			
OFFICIANT'S FEE	175			
NEW HOME (BUY/RENT)				
Related expenses				

Budgeted Items	Amount Budgeted	Total Cost	Deposit	Balance Due
Furniture	_____	_____	_____	_____
Related expenses		_____	_____	_____
		_____	_____	_____
		_____	_____	_____
		_____	_____	_____
		_____	_____	_____
		_____	_____	_____
		_____	_____	_____
Moving Costs	_____	_____	_____	_____
Related expenses		_____	_____	_____
		_____	_____	_____
		_____	_____	_____
		_____	_____	_____
		_____	_____	_____
		_____	_____	_____
		_____	_____	_____
Other	_____	_____	_____	_____
	_____	_____	_____	_____
	_____	_____	_____	_____
	_____	_____	_____	_____
	_____	_____	_____	_____
	_____	_____	_____	_____

The Ceremony

SETTING THE STYLE, DATE, TIME, AND LOCATION HOW-TO

- Before many decisions can be made, you and your fiancé will need to decide if the wedding will be formal or informal, large or small, and when and where it will take place.

- The style of the ceremony should be carried over to the reception.

- When regional or ethnic customs need to be observed, you may flavor your wedding by using one or two songs, by integrating colors in decorations or flowers, or by serving ethnic dishes compatible with other foods chosen for your reception.

- A formal wedding usually has these characteristics:

    —The bride wears a long, white or ivory gown with a chapel train and veil.

    —The bridesmaids wear floor-length gowns.

    —The groom and his attendants wear formal attire.

    —The bride's attendants include a maid or matron of honor, five to ten bridesmaids, and a flower girl.

    —The groom's attendants include a best man, one usher for every fifty guests (or one usher for each bridesmaid), and a ring bearer.

    —The ceremony takes place at a church, synagogue, large home, or garden.

    —The invitations and announcements are engraved.

- A semiformal wedding usually has these characteristics:

    —The bride wears a long, white or ivory gown with a short train and veil.

    —The bridesmaids wear floor-length gowns or a current style of dress.

    —The groom and his attendants wear tuxedos.

    —The bride's attendants include a maid or matron of honor and three to seven bridesmaids; a flower girl is optional.

—The groom's attendants include a best man and one usher for every fifty guests (or one for each bridesmaid); a ring bearer is optional.

—The ceremony takes place at a church, synagogue, chapel, home, garden, or hotel.

—The invitations and announcements are engraved or thermographed.

- An informal wedding usually has these characteristics:

—The bride wears a white or pastel dress or suit.

—The bridesmaid wears a dress complementary to the bride's dress.

—The groom and his attendant wear well-groomed suits.

—The bride's attendant is a maid or matron of honor.

—The groom's attendant is a best man (an usher is selected, if needed to seat guests).

—The ceremony usually takes place at a chapel, garden, home, or hotel.

—The invitations are handwritten or verbal.

- The time of your wedding should be compatible with the weather in your area. If your wedding is during the summer or in a warm area of the country, it may be wise to schedule the wedding for early in the morning or in the evening. Likewise, weddings in cold, winter climates would be better scheduled at midday or early afternoon.

- Have a few dates in mind before meeting with your officiant to select a wedding date.

- Verify these dates with possible reception sites before making your final choice.

- Second-time brides are freer today to choose the style of wedding and reception they desire, but in no way should a second wedding be seen as competing with the first.

- If this is a second marriage and you are considering a religious ceremony, you may need to inquire for a church and a clergy member willing to perform the wedding service.

- Unless military regulations stipulate otherwise, all officers have a choice whether to have a military wedding or civilian wedding.

  —Military weddings usually are held in a church or chapel. Military weddings are formal, with military personnel in full-dress uniform, including medals. Civilian members of the wedding party dress in complementary formal attire.

  —In a military wedding, the bridal couple usually walks through an arch of swords/sabers in the recessional as they exit the building. Other aspects of a military wedding are essentially the same as in any other wedding.

  —If you have questions regarding military traditions to be followed, or any other aspect of a military wedding, consult with an officer of protocol or commanding officer.

STYLE, DATE, TIME, AND LOCATION

1. Style of wedding: ☐ Formal ☒ Semiformal ☐ Informal
2. Day of week: 1st Choice _____ 2nd Choice _____
3. Time of day: (morning, afternoon, evening):

   1st Choice _____ 2nd Choice _____ 3rd Choice _____
4. Desired wedding date: _____

   Other possible dates: _____
5. Approximate number of guests: _____
6. Number of attendants: Bride: _____ Groom: _____
7. Color scheme: _____
8. Ceremony site:

   ☐ Church _____

   ☐ Synagogue _____

   ☐ Home _____ ☐ Garden _____

   ☐ Hotel _____

   ☐ Other (Such as private clubs, parks, rental halls, ships, museums)

   _____
9. Officiant: ☐ Clergy _____ ☐ Rabbi _____

   ☐ Judge _____ ☐ Justice _____
10. Reception site:

    ☐ Church _____

    ☐ Hotel _____

    ☐ Club _____

    ☐ Home _____ ☐ Garden _____

    ☐ Other _____
11. Customs and traditions to be observed: _____

    _____

    _____

    _____

    _____

OFFICIANT SELECTION

Option #1:

Name _____ Phone _____

Address _____

Appointment: Date _____ Time _____

Notes: _____

_____

_____

_____

_____

_____

_____

Fee: _____

Choice: ❑ Yes ❑ No   Date confirmed _____

Option #2:

Name _____ Phone _____

Address _____

Appointment: Date _____ Time _____

Notes: _____

_____

_____

_____

_____

_____

_____

Fee: _____

Choice: ❑ Yes ❑ No   Date confirmed _____

Premarital Counseling Schedule

Dates: _____ Times: _____

Location: _____

CEREMONY SITE

Option #1:

Site _____

Address _____

Contact person _____ Phone_____

	WEDDING	REHEARSAL
Available dates	_____	_____
Time preference	_____	_____
Confirmed	_____	_____

QUESTIONS ABOUT FACILITIES AND REGULATIONS:

1. How many guests can the site accommodate?_____

2. When is the site available for rehearsal?_____

3. What are the church requirements for marriage?_____

4. What, if any, are the regulations concerning the day or time of day to hold the wedding? _____

5. Do special vows need to be approved? ❑ Yes ❑ No

6. Is permission required   a) to marry in case of divorce? ❑ Yes ❑ No
    b) for a marriage of mixed religions? ❑ Yes ❑ No

7. What are the music restrictions?_____

8. What are the restrictions on decorations?_____
    Flowers?_____
    Throwing of rice/birdseed/confetti?_____

9. What accessories does the site provide and what are the fees for using these accessories?
    ❑ Candelabra $_____ ❑ Candles $_____ ❑ Candlelighters $_____
    ❑ Arch $_____ ❑ Kneeling bench $_____ ❑ Flower stands $_____
    ❑ Guest book stand $_____

10. What are the rules regarding photography?_____
    _____

11. Is there a designated room for the photographer to take pictures? ❑ Yes ❑ No

12. Is there a sound system for recording the wedding? ❑ Yes ❑ No
    Fee for use? $_____ Cost for copies? $_____

13. Are there facilities for the bridal party? ❑ Yes ❑ No Restrooms? ❑ Yes ❑ No
    Designated room for the bride? ❑ Yes ❑ No

14. What is the fee for the use of the building? $_____ For the custodian? $_____

15. What are the additional charges for using the site for the reception? $_____
    Notes:_____
    _____

Option #2:

Site _____

Address _____

Contact person _____ Phone_____

	WEDDING	REHEARSAL
Available dates	_____	_____
Time preference	_____	_____
Confirmed	_____	_____

QUESTIONS ABOUT FACILITIES AND REGULATIONS:

1. How many guests can the site accommodate?_____

2. When is the site available for rehearsal?_____

3. What are the church requirements for marriage?_____

4. What, if any, are the regulations concerning the day or time of day to hold the wedding? _____

5. Do special vows need to be approved? ❑ Yes ❑ No

6. Is permission required   a) to marry in case of divorce? ❑ Yes ❑ No
                  b) for a marriage of mixed religions? ❑ Yes ❑ No

7. What are the music restrictions?_____

8. What are the restrictions on decorations?_____
Flowers?_____
Throwing of rice/birdseed/confetti?_____

9. What accessories does the site provide and what are the fees for using these accessories?
❑ Candelabra $_____ ❑ Candles $_____ ❑ Candlelighters $_____
❑ Arch $_____ ❑ Kneeling bench $_____ ❑ Flower stands $_____
❑ Guest book stand $_____

10. What are the rules regarding photography?_____
_____

11. Is there a designated room for the photographer to take pictures? ❑ Yes ❑ No

12. Is there a sound system for recording the wedding? ❑ Yes ❑ No
Fee for use? $_____ Cost for copies? $_____

13. Are there facilities for the bridal party? ❑ Yes ❑ No Restrooms? ❑ Yes ❑ No
Designated room for the bride? ❑ Yes ❑ No

14. What is the fee for the use of the building? $_____ For the custodian? $_____

15. What are the additional charges for using the site for the reception? $_____
Notes:_____
_____

THE CEREMONY
HOW-TO

- The ceremony is the most important part of your wedding day.

- It is the position of the officiant (clergy, rabbi, or judge) that determines if the wedding is religious or civil.

- The order of the ceremony is often influenced by the customs and traditions of the area in which you live.

Religious Ceremonies

- A religious ceremony does not necessarily take place in a church or synagogue. Most officiants will perform a religious ceremony in the location of your choice.

- Use the ceremonial formats appropriate to your faith and to the religious traditions observed at your ceremony site.

Civil Ceremonies

- Most judges and justices are willing to perform the ceremony at the site of your choice if prior arrangements are made.

- The civil ceremony can be enhanced with music, decorations, and flowers.

The Prelude

- The organist or other instrumentalist could begin playing fifteen to thirty minutes before the start of the ceremony. The starting time depends upon the arrival of the guests.

- The candlelighting can take place anytime before the honor seating occurs.

- The bride's guests sit on the left side and the groom's guests sit on the right side. (In Jewish weddings, the seating is reversed.)

- If more guests have been seated on one side, the ushers should even out the seating during the last fifteen minutes prior to the ceremony.

- If parents are divorced, the father and mother can both sit on the front row if they are agreeable. If the father has remarried, he sits in the third row with his new wife; the mother still sits on the first row.

- The special (honor) seating is usually reserved only for parents and grandparents, but others who have been special to you may be included.

- The honor seating takes place just prior to the start of the ceremony in the order as follows: special guests, the groom's grandparents, the bride's grandparents, the groom's parents, the bride's mother.

- The bride's and groom's mothers may be escorted by specially appointed ushers, by their son or sons (one son on each arm), or by the groom himself.

- After the bride's mother is seated, aisle ribbons, if used, are drawn up the center aisle and across the end pews of the unreserved seating area.

- The two ushers who draw the aisle ribbons then unroll the aisle runner up the aisle from the foot of the wedding altar.

- The aisle ribbons and runner could already be in place before the guests arrive. The guests would then be escorted down the outer aisles to their seats.

The Processional

- The organist begins playing the selected music for the processional.

- Today's brides generally ask those participating in the processional to start off on the same foot, to walk with a slow, natural step, and to maintain an equal distance from the attendant who precedes them down the aisle.

- When you are about to enter, the organist increases the volume of the music being played. At this time, the organist could also change to another selection of music.

- Your mother may rise as you enter, a cue for all others to rise and remain standing until seated by the officiant.

- You may be escorted by your father, another close male relative, or a special friend.

- You may wait until the others have reached the altar before making your entrance, or you can double the distance between you and the preceding attendant before starting down the aisle.

- The organist stops playing when you reach the altar.

- For Jewish weddings, refer to the diagrams on page 75. The order of the processional and recessional and the positions under the chuppah are set by local custom.

The Ceremony

- Throughout the ceremony the bride and groom follow the leading of the officiant.

- The custom of giving away the bride is optional. In some services, after escorting the bride to the altar the father simply takes his seat alongside his wife. In others, the officiant asks, "Who gives this woman...?" The father may respond, "I do," or "Her mother and I do," or "We do."

- You relinquish your father's arm, hand your bouquet to your maid/matron of honor, and give your right arm to the groom.

- The wedding rings may be attached to the ring bearer's pillow by tying them with ribbon bows or by securing them with light stitches. It's better, however, for the best man and/or maid of honor to hold the rings until the appropriate time.

- The groom assists you as you move about the altar area—up and down any steps, kneeling and rising.

- Your maid of honor rearranges your train when appropriate and returns the bridal bouquet prior to the recessional.

- You and your fiancé may choose to write your own wedding vows. Use the Wording for Vows and Ring Ceremony to guide you as you write.

- After the pronouncement and blessing, the officiant may introduce the newly married couple to the wedding guests as Mr. and Mrs. _____.

- For an example of the ceremony order, see Worksheet 6 (page 60). This example is given only as a guide for planning; the officiant or his or her representative has the final word on the order to be observed, including any customs and traditions.

- As a token of your love and appreciation, you and the groom may elect to give your mothers roses at the start or close of the ceremony. The roses can be given in two ways:

  —You and the groom can each give a rose to your respective mothers.

  —You can give a rose to the groom's mother, and the groom can give one to your mother.

- You may decide to have a unity candle as part of the service.

  —The unity candle or Christ candle is a symbol of the bride and groom—once separate entities, now coming together as one in Christ.

  —The candelabra holds three candles. The outer two may be lit by the ushers during the candlelighting. At the designated time in the ceremony, the bride and groom each take one of the outer candles and together light the middle candle, after which the outer candles are extinguished by the groom.

  —To add a special touch, the mothers, after being escorted in, could individually light the candle representative of their child. Or you can have both sets of parents join in the lighting of the outer candles, symbolizing the union of two families.

- Communion (the Eucharist) could also be observed by the bride and groom only, or by all who wish to partake as part of the wedding ceremony.

- The officiant could invite both sets of parents to come forward to receive the new family member, and to promise to encourage you in your new marriage.

- Both fathers could offer prayers for you and the groom, asking God's blessing upon your marriage.

- The groom could offer a prayer, either following Communion or after lighting the unity candle.

- The honor attendants may offer special prayers or blessings for the bridal couple.

- Appropriate passages of Scripture could be read by your parents, attendants, or other family members and friends.

- Special letters from both your parents could be read by the best man and maid of honor.

- The guests might join in singing one or two verses of an appropriate hymn. Have all members of the bridal party, including the officiant, memorize the song or have them refrain from singing. If the officiant is leading the song, make certain he has a copy of the words.

- If you are planning a Jewish wedding, consult with the rabbi or synagogue of your choice on the ceremony order. The following example is given only as a guide to planning the order of a Jewish ceremony:

  —*processional*

  —*greeting:* Traditionally the rabbi extends a welcome to the bride and groom and their guests.

  —*invocation:* The rabbi offers a prayer for God's presence and His blessing on the marriage.

  —*first cup of wine, with a betrothal blessing:* The first cup of wine is lifted by the bride and groom to signify their betrothal; they may share this cup with their family and close friends.

  —*vows:* These may either precede or follow the ring ceremony.

  —*ring ceremony:* This may be either a single- or double-ring ceremony.

  —*reading of the ketubah:* The ketubah is the document giving the date and place of the wedding, the names of the bride and groom and their families, and any particulars concerning the marriage; it is much like a marriage contract, though now more only in form than in substance.

  —*second cup of wine (or the first cup filled and blessed a second time):* This cup signifies the nuptial ceremony; the rabbi may take a sip before first handing it to the groom, and then to the bride.

  —*lifting of the veil:* The veil is lifted by the bride's mother or a special friend.

  —*special presentations:* This could be music, poems, prayers, etc., shared by family and/or friends.

—*seven marriage blessings:* These may be chanted or read by the rabbi both in Hebrew and English; the bridal couple may select special guests to participate in the chanting and reading.

—*pronouncement*

—*benediction*

—*the broken glass:* "Mazel tov!"

—*recessional*

—*yichud:* After they leave the chuppah, the bride and groom traditionally spend ten to fifteen minutes alone in a separate room. It's a time to catch their breath, embrace, and share their first meal together, breaking their fast. Afterward they are greeted with a toast, singing and dancing, and a shower of rice.

The Recessional

• At the close of the ceremony, the organist or other instrumentalist begins playing the music for the recessional.

• The bride takes the groom's right arm as they lead the recessional.

• Other guests remain seated until the mothers and honored guests have been ushered out. Honored guests are ushered out in this order:

—the bride's mother and father

—the groom's mother and father

—the bride's grandparents

—the groom's grandparents

—any others

• After honored guests have been ushered out, the wedding officiant may make an announcement of:

—where and when the reception is to be held, and that everyone is invited.

—where the receiving line, if any, will be formed.

—how the guests are to be dismissed.

- Aisle ribbons, if used, are then removed from the unreserved seating areas, and two ushers standing in the main aisle dismiss guests by rows (or the guests may leave corporately).

- At weddings of less than 250 guests, the bride and groom may return after the parents and grandparents have been ushered out to greet and dismiss their guests individually and by rows. This may be done in lieu of a receiving line.

- Special music, either vocal or instrumental, can also be included during the postlude as the guests are being dismissed, especially at large weddings or when the bride and groom are dismissing the guests themselves.

- For Jewish weddings, refer to page 75.

- As a part of the recessional in a military wedding, the ushers (military officers) draw their swords/sabers and form the arch under which the bridal couple pass. The arch may be formed inside the church at the foot of the altar steps, or outside the church either at the door or on the steps. The arch may also be formed both inside and outside, depending on the church rules and the particular branch of the service.

  When the arch is formed inside, the ushers take their places, facing each other, and on command form the arch. The bride and groom pass through as they walk up the aisle. They are followed by the maid/matron of honor and the best man, then the bridesmaids in twos, with the ushers exiting through a side door to form the arch again outside. Or, once the bride and groom have passed through the arch, the ushers may sheath their swords/sabers and escort the bridesmaids up the aisle.

  When the arch is formed outside the church, the bride and groom and their remaining attendants wait in the vestibule until the ushers are in place. The parents and honored guests are escorted from the church in the usual manner and take their positions outside. The rest of the guests are then ushered out to join them. As the bridal couple arrives at the entrance, the head usher gives the command "Draw swords" or "Draw sabers." Each usher raises his sword/saber in his right hand with the cutting edge on top. After the bride and groom have passed through the arch, the command is given to "Return Swords" or "Return Sabers." Once this last order is given, the remaining attendants follow the bride and groom outside.

CEREMONY ORDER

Prelude _____

_____

Special music _____

_____

Processional _____

_____

Presentation of the bride _____

_____

Special music/prayer/reading _____

_____

Wedding message by officiant _____

_____

Exchange of vows and rings _____

_____

Communion _____

_____

Lighting of unity candle _____

_____

Special music/prayer/reading _____

_____

Pronouncement/declaration _____

_____

Benediction/blessing _____

_____

Kiss _____

_____

Presentation _____

_____

Postlude _____

_____

WORDING FOR VOWS AND RING CEREMONY

Vows of the Groom to the Bride

_____
_____
_____
_____
_____
_____
_____
_____

Vows of the Bride to the Groom

_____
_____
_____
_____
_____
_____
_____
_____

Ring Ceremony

_____
_____
_____
_____
_____
_____
_____

WEDDING COORDINATOR HOW-TO

- Wedding coordinators are available to orchestrate the varied details associated with a successful wedding and reception.

- The cost of a coordinator varies greatly and depends largely on the amount of time spent on your wedding.

- By using the *Complete Wedding Planner* you can handle the wedding preliminaries yourself, but it is still wise to have a coordinator to help keep your wedding day organized.

- A coordinator can smooth the wedding day's progression and so help provide the relaxed and enjoyable day you desire.

- A relative or close friend may be able to do the wedding day coordinating for you.

- Many churches have wedding hostesses who know about church facilities and policies.

- During the planning process, have the person designated to coordinate your wedding day use the Wedding and Rehearsal Information List on pages 66–70, and perhaps the Reception Organizer on pages 130–31. These pages may be filled out, photocopied, and given to the wedding coordinator.

- Additional tips for the wedding coordinator:

  —Acquaint yourself with the ceremony site.

  —Discuss with the bride and groom any wedding policies of the ceremony site.

  —Be available to assist the bride and groom by answering questions, offering suggestions, and having names of available resources for services.

  —Be as organized as possible, with all wedding day information in one place.

  —As you assist the bridal couple in planning their big day, know the following:
    (1) Who will be giving the bride away?
    (2) Will the bridal couple be having a double-ring ceremony? Who will have the rings?

(3) Will the officiant provide the wording for the vows, or will the bride and groom be writing their own?

(4) Will Communion (the Eucharist) be observed? Who will participate?

(5) Will the lighting of the unity candle be included?

(6) What other special observances will be a part of the ceremony?

(7) Who will have the marriage license? When and where will it be signed?

(8) Will the bridal couple have a receiving line? If so, where? Who will be involved?

(9) Who will be responsible for any audio and/or videotapes of the ceremony? of the reception?

(10) Who will be responsible for cleaning out the bride's dressing room? The groom's dressing room?

(11) If a preceremony buffet is to be served at the ceremony site, who will be responsible for setup? serving? cleanup?

(12) Where will the reception be? How soon will it follow the ceremony?

(13) Who will be responsible for taking the guest book to the reception? To whose home afterward?

(14) Who will be responsible for transporting the gifts from the ceremony site? from the reception site? To whose house?

—Confirm your arrival time for both the rehearsal and ceremony with the custodian of the facility (or other designated person). This time should be early enough to accomplish any necessary advance preparations: unlocking doors, setting up equipment and accessories, turning on lights, heating or air conditioning, etc.

—Confirm with the bride the arrival times of the bridal party, the bride's and groom's parents, grandparents, special others, the officiant(s), musicians, florist, photographer, etc. On the wedding day be available to greet each one, to answer any questions, and to give any last-minute instructions.

—At the rehearsal, review the wedding day arrival times with the participants— who's to be where and when—and indicate to them the importance of being on time.

—If possible, have all the decisions concerning the ceremony made prior to the rehearsal. If any unexpected changes do occur, they should quickly be addressed to the bride.

—Make certain that each of the ushers receives a list of his responsibilities at the ceremony site ("Responsibilities of the Ushers," page 99–101). Also, take time at the rehearsal to demonstrate exactly how they are to usher, and allow them to practice. Don't assume they already know what to do.

—As the wedding coordinator you will probably be responsible for collecting any fees or honorariums from the bride and groom. These may be disbursed either at the rehearsal, before the ceremony, or after the reception, as previously indicated by the recipients.

—Determine how many seats (or pews) need to be reserved for special seating, and who will be sitting where.

—Before the florist leaves the premises on the wedding day, count the bouquets, boutonnieres, and corsages to make certain all the needed flowers are there.

—Know when and where the photographer will be taking pictures.

—When an aisle runner is being used, make certain it has been firmly pinned and taped in place. Tape the end of the runner down once it has been pulled up the aisle to keep it taut.

—If the facility is not equipped with a signaling system, a small flashlight may be used to cue the musicians for the start of the processional and for any other special timing needs.

—Be prepared for possible emergencies with a special bag that includes these items: aspirin, breath mints, clear nail polish, emery boards, facial tissues, hair spray, iron, sanitary napkins, scissors, sewing kit, spot remover, static spray, and straight and safety pins.

—Another bag may contain: pins (for flowers and for pinning the aisle runner in place), small flashlight (for signaling musicians), hair dryer (for hair needs and candle wax removal), masking tape (for marking the positions of the bridal party), matches or lighter (for lighting candles or candlelighters), measuring tape (for locating positions of the bridal party), scotch tape (for taping gift cards to packages), black ink pens (for signing the marriage license).

ESTIMATE FOR WEDDING COORDINATOR

Name _____ Phone _____

Address _____

Appointment: Date _____ Time _____

Fee is based on:

   ❑ Percentage _____   ❑ Hourly rate _____

   ❑ Per guest _____   ❑ Flat fee _____

Number of hours needed _____

Services_____

_____

_____

_____

_____

_____

_____

_____

_____

_____

Choice: Total cost $_____

❑ Yes   ❑ No   Deposit $_____

Date confirmed _____   Balance due $_____

Planning schedule:

DATE	TIME	PLANNING TOPIC
_____	_____	_____
_____	_____	_____
_____	_____	_____
_____	_____	_____

WEDDING COORDINATOR'S INFORMATION LIST

1. Bride _____ Phone: *Home* _____ *Work* _____
   Groom _____ Phone: *Home* _____ *Work* _____
   Bride's parents _____ Phone: *Home* _____ *Work* _____
   Groom's parents _____ Phone: *Home* _____ *Work* _____

2. Wedding date _____ Time _____
   Number of guests _____
   Rehearsal date _____ Time _____

3. Officiant(s) _____ Phone _____
   _____ Phone _____

4. Ceremony site
   Contact person _____ Phone _____
   Custodian _____ Phone _____

5. Wedding color scheme _____
   Style of wedding _____

6. Bride's attendants:
   Maid/Matron of honor _____ Phone _____
   Bridesmaids _____ Phone _____
   _____ Phone _____
   _____ Phone _____
   _____ Phone _____
   _____ Phone _____
   Flower girl _____ Phone _____
   Bride and Attendants ❑ Dress at home
                         ❑ Dress at ceremony site (room _____)
   Arrival time: Rehearsal _____ Wedding _____

7. Groom's attendants:
   Best man _____ Phone _____
   Head usher _____ Phone _____
   Ushers _____ Phone _____
   _____ Phone _____
   _____ Phone _____

Ring bearer _____ Phone _____

Groom and attendants   ❏ Dress at home

                      ❏ Dress at ceremony site (room _____)

Arrival time: Rehearsal _____ Wedding _____

8. Musicians:

Organist _____ Phone _____

Soloists _____ Phone _____

_____ Phone _____

Other musicians _____ Phone _____

_____ Phone _____

Arrival time: Rehearsal _____ Wedding _____ Set-up Room _____

(See Musicians' Needs Checklist, page 149)

9. Florist _____ Phone _____

Arrival time _____

Supplier of Wedding Accessories	Ceremony Site	Florist:	Rental Equipment
Arch or Canopy	❏	❏	❏
Altar candelabra	❏	❏	❏
Pew candelabra	❏	❏	❏
Unity candelabra	❏	❏	❏
Candles (quantity___)	❏	❏	❏
Candlelighters (quantity___)	❏	❏	❏
Kneeling bench	❏	❏	❏
Aisle runner (length ___)	❏	❏	❏
Guest book stand or table	❏	❏	❏
Gift table	❏	❏	❏
Other	❏	❏	❏

(For placement of flowers, wedding accessories, and aisle runner, see the diagrams on page 158)

Persons receiving special corsages   Persons receiving special boutonnieres

_____   _____

_____   _____

_____   _____

_____   _____

10. Photographer _____ Phone _____

     Arrival time _____ Room _____

Time when pictures are to be taken _____

11. Video operator _____ Phone _____

     Arrival time _____

     Audio operator_____ Phone _____

     Arrival time _____

(See Video and Audio Planning Worksheets on pages 170, 172)

12. Guest book attendants _____ Phone _____

     _____ Phone _____

     Arrival time _____

     Gift attendant _____ Phone _____

     Arrival time _____

13. Wedding day transportation

     Contact person _____ Phone _____

14. If reception is being held at the ceremony site:

     Caterer _____ Phone _____

     Arrival time _____

     Bakery _____ Phone _____

     Arrival time _____

     Rental equipment _____ Phone _____

     Arrival time _____

15. Reception hostess _____ Phone _____

16. Ceremony order and timing: Preceremony ushering begins _____

Candlelighting

TIME	TYPE		USHER
_____	Pew candles		_____
_____	Candelabra		_____
_____	Unity candelabra		_____
_____	Other _____		_____

Special Seating

TIME	WHO	WHICH PEW	USHER
_____	_____	_____	_____
_____	_____	_____	_____
_____	_____	_____	_____
_____	Mother of the groom	_____	_____
_____	Mother of the bride	_____	_____

Aisle Ribbons and Runner

TIME	AISLE TO BE USED	USHERS
_____	_____	_____

Special Music

TIME	WHO
_____	_____
_____	_____

Processional Order (beginning time _____)

_____	_____
_____	_____
_____	_____
_____	_____

Recessional Order

_____	_____
_____	_____
_____	_____
_____	_____

Postlude

_____

Order of Dismissal of Special Guests

_____   _____

_____   _____

_____   _____

_____   _____

Removal of Aisle Ribbons
Ushers _____

Dismissal of Remaining Guests
Ushers _____

THE REHEARSAL
HOW-TO

- The rehearsal is generally held the day before the wedding.

- In the case of small, intimate weddings, the rehearsal may consist of only a few minutes of instruction prior to the ceremony.

- The rehearsal allows the participants the opportunity to practice specific duties—ushering, lighting of the candles, entrances and exits, special cues, variations in the service, and so on.

- The people required to attend the rehearsal are the officiant or his or her representative, the bride and groom, their parents, and all the bridal attendants. Musicians and soloists may or may not attend.

- Confer with the officiant concerning any last-minute changes in the order of the ceremony.

- Make certain the officiant can correctly pronounce the names of the bride and groom.

- It's best to have only one person conduct the rehearsal. However, your officiant and wedding coordinator may work together, each being responsible for different portions of the rehearsal.

- You and your bridal attendants may use ribbon bouquets from your showers to practice carrying bouquets.

- When the musicians are present, they should perform enough of each selection so that everyone is acquainted with the music and aware of any necessary cues.

- Bring the following items to the rehearsal:

  —cellophane tape (two dispensers) for taping cards to gift packages

  —guest book and pens

  —ribbon bouquets

  —programs

Rehearsal Information List

The rehearsal should begin with the bridal party taking their positions at the wedding altar. Once all the participants know where to stand, they can be instructed on how to reach that position.

Diagram of Altar Positions

Diagram of Processional

Diagram of Recessional

Type of step used in the processional _____

Distance between participants during processional _____

Special Cues

Mothers' seating_____

_____

Entry of bridal party_____

_____

Bride's mother rises _____

Ring bearer and flower girl after reaching altar will

     ❑ Remain with bridal party   ❑ Be seated with parents

Father's response _____

_____

Other _____

Variations in the Service

Special acknowledgment of parents _____

Kiss or embrace _____ By whom?_____

When? _____

Mothers' roses ❑ Yes ❑ No By whom? _____

When? _____

Unity candle ❑ Yes ❑ No When?_____

Lifting of blusher veil? ❑ Yes ❑ No By whom? _____

When? ❑ Yes ❑ No By whom? _____

Other ❑ Yes ❑ No By whom? _____

Ushers' Postceremony Duties

Removal of any flowers to reception site ❑ Yes ❑ No

  By whom? _____

Removal of bridal party apparel from ceremony site ❑ Yes ❑ No

  By whom? _____

POSITION DIAGRAMS

(Christian Ceremony)

B=Bride   G=Groom   O=Officiant   MH=Maid (or Matron) of Honor

BM=Best Man   Bm=Bridesmaids   U=Ushers   fg=flower girl

rb=ring bearer   FB=Father of the Bride   HU=Head Usher

In the Processional

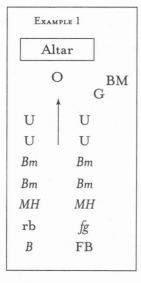 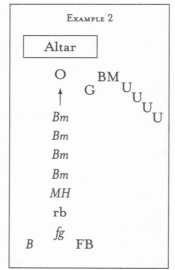

In the Recessional

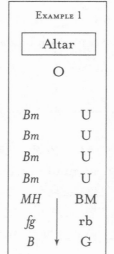 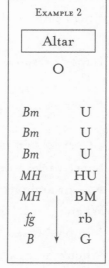

At the Altar

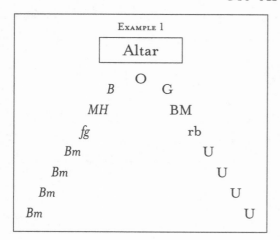 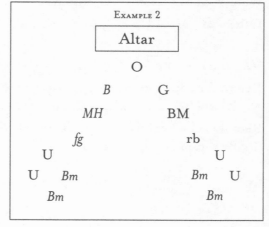

74

POSITION DIAGRAMS

(Jewish Ceremony)

B=Bride   G=Groom   R/C=Rabbi and/or Cantor

MH=Maid (or Matron) of Honor   BM=Best Man

Bm=Bridesmaids   U=Ushers   fg/rb=flower girl/ring bearer

FB=Father of the Bride   MB=Mother of the Bride

FG=Father of the Groom   MG=Mother of the Groom

BGf=Bride's Grandfather   BGm=Bride's Grandmother

GGf=Groom's Grandfather   GGm=Groom's Grandmother

In the Processional

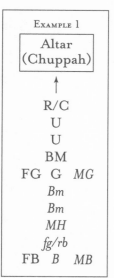

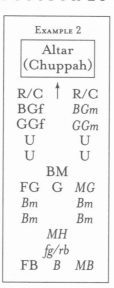

In the Recessional

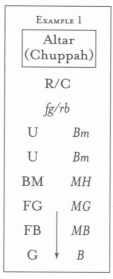

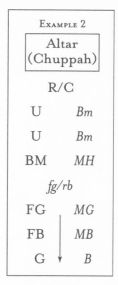

Under the Chuppah

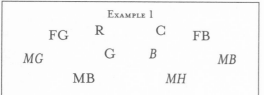

Note: When room permits, grandparents may join the Bride, Groom, Honor Attendants, Parents, Rabbi and Cantor under the Chuppah.

Note: The Bridesmaids, Ushers, Flower Girl, and Ring Bearer do not stand under the Chuppah.

Attire and Attendants

BRIDAL ATTIRE
HOW-TO

- Use the Wedding Gown Search List to keep track of designs, styles, and costs of gowns that interest you.

- It usually takes twelve to sixteen weeks from the time the manufacturer cuts the fabric until the gown is delivered to the store.

- Give the manufacturer a target date that allows ample time for alterations and formal photographs before your wedding day.

- If you need extra fabric to cover a headpiece, for special alterations, or to dress a miniature replica of the bride, it should be ordered at the same time as your gown.

- Generally, once an order has been placed the gown must be purchased, even if your circumstances change.

- Many stores require a 50 percent deposit when you order your gown.

- It's best to select the headpiece and veil when you select your gown. (If you must buy at another time, try the veil on with the same style of gown or one of similar styling to see how it will look.) Select a headpiece that complements both your gown and your hairstyle.

- Consider ordering your headpiece with a detachable veil. The veil can be removed for the reception, thereby eliminating having your headpiece tugged and pulled by well-wishers.

- When gloves are worn, the underseam of the glove's ring finger is slit so that the ring may be placed on your finger

- Wear your engagement ring on the ring finger of your right hand during the ceremony. Then place it in front of your wedding ring once the ceremony is over.

- Any other jewelry should not detract from the overall effect you desire.

- White satin, lace, or fine leather shoes are usually worn. Heel height is a matter of choice.

- Because of the length of time you'll need to be wearing your shoes, it's important to carefully break them in before the wedding day.

- Your wedding lingerie will be determined by the style of gown you select. The bridal salesperson should be able to advise you in your choice.

- Don't plan your final fitting too early. With all your involvement in prewedding activities, you may find yourself gaining or losing weight.

- For the fittings, wear the lingerie and shoes you'll be wearing for your wedding.

- If this is your second marriage, there are many beautiful gowns available from tea length to the more traditional style. You may choose white, but a light pastel shade is often chosen.

- It is customary for the bride or her mother to make suggestions to the groom's mother about her outfit—the length of dress, length of sleeves, color, and style.

- The mothers' dresses should be similar in style, and consistent with the style of the wedding (floor-length for formal, floor-length or tea-length for semiformal, street-length dress or suit for informal). Colors should complement both the bride's color and each other.

- Due to the emphasis placed on the bride, many mothers wait too late to order a dress, and often end up with make-do selections. This is both unnecessary and regrettable, because the mothers are in the spotlight too.

- A bride who is in the military may choose to wear either her dress uniform or a traditional wedding gown.

WEDDING GOWN
SEARCH LIST

Description _____

    Manufacturer _____ Style # _____

    Cost _____

    Store _____

    Contact person _____ Phone _____

Description _____

    Manufacturer _____ Style # _____

    Cost _____

    Store _____

    Contact person _____ Phone _____

Description _____

    Manufacturer _____ Style # _____

    Cost _____

    Store _____

    Contact person _____ Phone _____

Description _____

    Manufacturer _____ Style # _____

    Cost _____

    Store _____

    Contact person _____ Phone _____

Description _____

    Manufacturer _____ Style # _____

    Cost _____

    Store _____

    Contact person _____ Phone _____

Description _____

    Manufacturer _____ Style # _____

    Cost _____

    Store _____

    Contact person _____ Phone _____

BRIDAL ATTIRE

Bridal shop _____

Address _____

Contact person _____ Phone _____

Contract terms _____

Payment schedule _____

ITEM AND DESCRIPTION	COST	DEPOSIT	DUE
Wedding gown			
Manufacturer			
Style #			
Headpiece			
Manufacturer			
Style #			
Veil			
Manufacturer			
Style #			
Accessories			
Shoes			
Hosiery			
Slip			
Bra			
Gloves			
Jewelry			
Other			

Alterations

Fitting dates/Times _____/_____/_____/_____ Final _____/_____

Contact person _____ Phone _____

Address _____ Cost _____

Delivery

❑ Church ❑ Home ❑ Pick up date _____ Time_____

Pressing instructions _____

_____

Date needed for portrait _____

To heirloom gown:

Name _____

Address _____ Phone _____

Contact person _____ Date _____ Cost _____

TROUSSEAU INVENTORY

SUITS, DRESSES	SEPARATES: BLOUSES, PANTS, SKIRTS, SWEATERS	ACCESSORIES: SHOES, SCARVES, BELTS, JEWELRY
ITEMS TO BUY		

LINGERIE	SLEEPWEAR	MISCELLANEOUS: CLOTHING FOR SWIMMING, TENNIS, GOLF, ETC.
ITEMS TO BUY		

Bride's Honeymoon
Packing Checklist

Honeymoon Location _____

Dates _____ Climate _____

CLOTHING NEEDS

Lingerie/Sleepwear _____

_____

_____

_____

Casual/Sportswear _____

_____

_____

_____

_____

_____

Daytime _____

_____

_____

_____

_____

_____

Evening _____

_____

_____

_____

Accessories _____

_____

_____

Cosmetics, Medications _____

_____

_____

_____

Bride's Wedding Day Checklist

Item	Packed and Ready
Wedding Gown	❑
Headpiece and Veil	❑
Bra, Slip, Panties	❑
Hosiery, two pair	❑
Shoes	❑
Gloves	❑
Jewelry	❑
Makeup, Nail Polish	❑
Comb, Brush, Curling Iron	❑
Hairspray and Bobby Pins	❑
Mirror	❑
Sewing Kit	❑
Iron	❑
Other	❑

Clothes to Change into before Leaving Reception

Going-away Outfit

Bra

Slip

Hosiery

Shoes

Accessories

BRIDAL ATTENDANTS
HOW-TO

- Bridal attendants are chosen from your close friends and family members, including any sisters of the groom.

- You may elect to have both a maid and matron of honor, but you will have to designate which one will attend you at the altar, to hold your bouquet and the groom's ring, and to help with your veil and train.

- If you decide to have a flower girl, the best ages are between four and nine. If any are younger than this, be prepared for the unexpected to happen, because a younger child's actions can be very unpredictable. If you decide to have children in your wedding party who are under four years of age, you may want to have them seated with their parents once the officiant has asked, "Who gives this woman?" They can later follow the bride and groom back up the aisle during the recessional.

- Junior bridesmaids are generally between the ages of ten and sixteen.

- Bridesmaids are usually sixteen years of age and older.

- Special others can be included in the House Party by having them preside over the guest book and gift tables, distribute rice, serve the cake and punch, entertain the guests, provide housing and transportation, or cover various details for you.

- When a remarriage occurs and there are children involved (yours, the groom's, or both), give them all honored positions in the day's activities.
  If they are willing, you could have the children stand with you at the altar. Teenagers or adult children may serve as your honor attendants. Younger children could serve as flower girls or ring bearers. They could also escort you down the aisle. They can further participate in the ceremony by reading a special poem, Scripture, or prayer.
  When your plans involve children from former marriages, you may need to check with the other parent before involving them in your wedding activities.

- When selecting the bridal attendants' dresses and accessories, consider their financial status and if the dress will be useful to them afterward.

- If possible, have a couple of your attendants try on two or three different styles of dresses. It is nice to ask them for their opinion, but the final choice is yours.

- Order the dresses at the same time to avoid any variations in color and design.

- The flower girl's dress may be the same style as the bridesmaids', or a dress of complementary style and color. It may also be shorter in length for ease of movement.

- In some ceremony locations, your attendants may be required to have their heads covered; otherwise, the choice is yours.

- Attendants' shoes should be of the same style, but the height of the heels may vary according to the girls' heights and their individual need for comfort.

- If the attendants' shoes are being dyed to match, have them done at the same place and time to ensure color conformity.

- Select a complementary shade of hosiery and purchase two pairs for each attendant (an extra pair for emergencies).

- Any jewelry that is worn should be small and dainty, of the same or similar style.

- Any gloves that are worn should be of the same style and length.

- Use fabric swatches to coordinate colors of lipstick and nail polish for the attendants.

- For dresses other than floor-length, it's better to have the hems measured down from the knee of each bridesmaid rather than the same distance up from the floor. Just as the head heights of the girls vary, so should their hem lengths. The overall appearance of each girl in her dress is far more important than all dresses being the same distance from the floor.

- If possible, have everyone dress at the ceremony site to avoid wrinkling dresses in transit.

- Bridal attendants should be invited to all parties given for the bride or the bride and groom, including the rehearsal dinner. The only exceptions may be special group or office parties.

- The flower girl is not usually invited to the bridal parties, but her mother is. Her parents may be invited to any parties given for both the bride and groom, and her father to any bachelor parties. Invite the flower girl to the rehearsal dinner. If it's the night before the wedding, her parents may decide to have her forgo the dinner so she'll be rested for the wedding day.

- Your gifts to the bridesmaids are usually alike, but the honor attendant's gift may vary from the others in style and design. The flower girl may receive a different type of gift than the other attendants.

- Possible gift choices: for the bridesmaids—keepsake boxes, books, compacts, cosmetic bags, crystal, evening bags, engraved pen and pencil sets, jewelry, jewelry cases, perfume, photo albums, picture frames, porcelain, or stationery; for the flower girl—charm bracelet, china doll, jewelry box, piggy bank, or stuffed animal.

Responsibilities of the Maid/Matron of Honor

- Before the wedding, she
  —may help you in such ways as addressing invitations and entertaining out-of-town guests.
  —is responsible for making and keeping any alteration appointments.
  —should wear the lingerie and shoes she will be wearing for the wedding when she goes for fittings, to ensure a more perfect fit.
  —must attend the wedding rehearsal.
  —arrives early at a designated place to help you dress.

- During the ceremony, she
  —precedes you and your father in the processional.
  —arranges your train at the altar.
  —holds the bridal bouquet at the required time.

—may be in charge of the groom's ring in a double-ring ceremony until it is needed.

—adjusts your veil and again arranges your train for the recessional.

—usually walks with the best man in the recessional.

—signs the marriage license.

- At the reception, she

—stands next to the groom in the receiving line.

—sits on the groom's left during a sit-down meal.

—helps you change into your going-away clothes.

—informs the parents when the bridal couple is ready to leave.

Responsibilities of the Bridesmaids

- Before the wedding, they

—may help you address invitations and assist with any errands.

—are responsible for individually making and keeping their alteration appointments.

—should wear the lingerie and shoes they will be wearing for the wedding when they go for fittings, to ensure a more perfect fit.

—must attend the wedding rehearsal.

- During the ceremony, they

—either walk alone, in pairs, or with an usher in the processional.

—are usually escorted by the ushers in the recessional. When there are more bridesmaids than ushers, the extras can walk alone or in pairs.

- At the reception, they

—may stand in the receiving line.

—sit at either the bride's table or a special attendants' table during a sit-down or buffet dinner, seated in alternating positions with the ushers around the table.

—mingle with the guests, helping the hosts entertain.

Responsibilities of the Flower Girl

- Before the wedding, she

  —is responsible for making and keeping her alteration appointments.

  —should wear the lingerie and shoes she will be wearing for the wedding when she goes for fittings, to ensure a more perfect fit.

  —must attend the wedding rehearsal.

  —may attend the rehearsal dinner along with her parents.

- During the ceremony, she

  —walks, alone or with the ring bearer, directly in front of you and your father in the processional.

  —may stand with the bridal party at the altar or be seated with her parents during the ceremony.

  —may follow directly behind the bride and groom in the recessional.

- At the reception, she

  —does not stand in the receiving line.

  —either remains with her parents or sits at a special table for children under adult supervision.

BRIDAL ATTENDANTS'
DRESSES AND ACCESSORIES

DRESS OPTION #1

Description _____

_____

    Manufacturer _____ Style # _____ Cost _____

    Store _____

    Address _____

    Contact person _____ Phone _____

DRESS OPTION #2

Description _____

_____

    Manufacturer _____ Style # _____ Cost _____

    Store _____

    Address _____

    Contact person _____ Phone _____

DRESS OPTION #3

Description _____

_____

    Manufacturer _____ Style # _____ Cost _____

    Store _____

    Address _____

    Contact person _____ Phone _____

DRESS CHOICE # _____ DATE ORDERED _____ DELIVERY DATE _____

ACCESSORIES

Shoes _____ Cost _____

Hosiery _____ Cost _____

Head covering _____ Cost _____

Jewelry _____ Cost _____

Makeup (lipstick, nail polish) _____ Cost _____

Other _____ Cost _____

BRIDAL ATTENDANTS LIST

Maid/Matron of Honor _____

Address _____ Phone _____

City _____ State _____ Zip _____

Sizes: Dress _____ Shoe _____ Hose _____ Glove _____ Head _____

Your Gift for Her _____

Bridesmaid _____

Address _____ Phone _____

City _____ State _____ Zip _____

Sizes: Dress _____ Shoe _____ Hose _____ Glove _____ Head _____

Your Gift for Her _____

Bridesmaid _____

Address _____ Phone _____

City _____ State _____ Zip _____

Sizes: Dress _____ Shoe _____ Hose _____ Glove _____ Head _____

Your Gift for Her _____

Bridesmaid _____

Address _____ Phone _____

City _____ State _____ Zip _____

Sizes: Dress _____ Shoe _____ Hose _____ Glove _____ Head _____

Your Gift for Her _____

Bridesmaid _____

Address _____ Phone _____

City _____ State _____ Zip _____

Sizes: Dress _____ Shoe _____ Hose _____ Glove _____ Head _____

Your Gift for Her _____

Bridesmaid _____

Address _____ Phone _____

City _____ State _____ Zip _____

Sizes: Dress _____ Shoe _____ Hose _____ Glove _____ Head _____

Your Gift for Her _____

Bridesmaid/Flower Girl _____

Address _____ Phone _____

City _____ State _____ Zip _____

Sizes: Dress _____ Shoe _____ Hose _____ Glove _____ Head _____

Your Gift for Her _____

BRIDAL ATTENDANTS' GUIDELINES

(for the week before the wedding)

- Carefully break in your shoes.
- Have final fittings, if necessary.
- Make sure you have everything you need—dress, shoes, hosiery, lingerie, gloves, jewelry, makeup, etc.
- Gather all essentials ahead of time and place in one area to avoid last-minute frazzled nerves while trying to find something you've forgotten.
- Get plenty of rest.

BRIDAL LUNCHEON

Location _____

Address _____

Date _____ Time _____ Phone _____

REHEARSAL AT CEREMONY SITE

Location _____

Address _____

Date _____ Time _____ Phone _____

REHEARSAL DINNER

Location _____

Address _____

Date _____ Time _____ Phone _____

ARRIVAL TIME AT THE WEDDING SITE FOR THE CEREMONY _____

WHERE TO DRESS _____

PHOTOGRAPHS

Location _____

Address _____

Date _____ Time _____ Phone _____

RECEPTION

Location _____

Address _____

Date _____ Time _____ Phone _____

TRANSPORTATION

To the ceremony site _____

To the reception site _____

OTHER _____

GROOM'S FORMAL ATTIRE

Style of Wedding _____

Color Scheme _____

Store _____

Address _____

Contact person _____ Phone _____

Groom's Sizes: Coat _____ Sleeve _____ Neck _____

Waist _____ Inseam _____ Shoe _____

	GROOM'S ATTIRE		ATTIRE FOR FATHERS & GROOM'S ATTENDANTS	
	OPTION #1	OPTION #2	OPTION #1	OPTION #2
Style				
Color				
Coat				
Trousers				
Shirt				
Vest				
Ties				
Ascot				
Cummerbund				
Dress socks				
Shoes				
Gloves				
Suspenders				
Studs and cuff links				
FINAL CHOICE(✓)	☐	☐	☐	☐
Total Cost				
Deposit				
Fitting date				
Pickup date				
Return date				

GROOM'S HONEYMOON PACKING CHECKLIST

Honeymoon Location _____

Dates _____ Climate _____

Underwear/Sleepwear _____

_____

_____

_____

Casual/Sportswear _____

_____

_____

_____

_____

Daytime _____

_____

_____

_____

_____

Evening _____

_____

_____

_____

Accessories _____

_____

_____

Toiletries, Medications _____

_____

_____

_____

GROOM'S WEDDING DAY CHECKLIST

ITEM	PACKED AND READY
Coat	❏
Trousers	❏
Shirt	❏
Vest	❏
Tie	❏
Ascot	❏
Cummerbund	❏
Shoes	❏
Gloves	❏
Suspenders	❏
Studs and cuff links	❏
Underwear	❏
Socks	❏
Handkerchief	❏
Toiletries	❏
Other	❏

Clothes to Change into before Leaving Reception

Jacket	❏
Slacks	❏
Shirt	❏
Tie	❏
Underwear	❏
Socks	❏
Shoes	❏
Accessories	❏

GROOM'S ATTENDANTS HOW-TO

- The best man is usually the groom's most trustworthy and faithful friend or relative.

- The ushers may be the groom's brothers, cousins, or best friends, or brothers and close relatives of the bride.

- The ring bearer, a young boy between the ages of four and nine (using anyone younger than four is not recommended, no matter how cute he is), is usually a relative of the bride or groom or the child of a dear friend.

- When all the groom's attendants live in the same town, they should all visit the same store to be measured and fitted for their formal attire. If someone lives out of town, he can be measured in the shop of his choice. He should then mail his correct measurements to the bride or groom, who will reserve formal wear and accessories for the final fitting.

- In a military wedding, the groom, as a member of the armed forces, chooses attendants from among his military friends. His best man, though, may be civilian.

- The arch of swords (navy) and sabers (army) is reserved only for officers. There should be a minimum of four sword/saber bearers, but it is better to have six or eight. The swords or sabers are not worn by the military ushers while seating guests, but are put on just prior to the processional.

- The groom's attendants are invited to attend all parties given for the bridal couple except possibly office or special group parties. They are also invited to all bachelor parties.

- You may invite the ring bearer to attend parties for the bride and groom, but because of his age his parents may have him forgo attending. But do invite his parents to attend. Also invite his mother to attend any bridal showers, and his father to attend any bachelor parties.

- The ushers' gifts should all be alike.

- The best man's gift may vary from the ushers' in style and design.

- A different kind of gift may be given to the ring bearer, one appropriate for his age.

- Possible gift choices: for the best man and ushers—belt buckles, billfolds, business card cases, collar stay collections, date books, desk accessories, hardbound books, jewelry cases, key rings, money clips, paperweights, pen and pencil sets, pewter mugs, picture frames, CDs/tapes, sports tickets, stationery, or travel clocks; and for the ring bearer—a board game, basketball, model airplane, monogrammed mug, or soccer ball.

Responsibilities of the Best Man

- Before the wedding, he

  —pays for his own attire, purchased or rented.

  —is responsible for making and keeping appointments for fittings.

  —tries on formal attire before the wedding, preferably before leaving the store in case any sizes need to be exchanged.

  —may confirm the honeymoon travel arrangements for the groom.

  —hosts the bachelor party if other arrangements have not been made.

  —helps the bride's mother with last-minute details.

  —attends the rehearsal and rehearsal dinner.

  —may help the groom finish packing.

  —may provide transportation to the ceremony site for the groom.

  —obtains the marriage license from the groom and holds it until the appropriate time for signing.

  —is in charge of the officiant's fee. May give the envelope to the officiant before the ceremony.

  —may also supervise the ushers, making sure they are thoroughly briefed, dressed, and at the ceremony site at the appropriate time.

- During the ceremony, he

  —is not part of the processional but enters with the groom, standing behind the groom and slightly to the left.

—may hold the wedding ring until the officiant asks for it.

—walks with the maid/matron of honor in the recessional.

- After the ceremony, he

—immediately serves as one of the witnesses in signing the marriage license.

—helps the bride and groom into their car or other form of transportation if the reception is being held at another location.

—may drive the bride and groom to the reception.

—usually drives the maid of honor and other bridesmaids to the reception.

- At the reception, he

—does not stand in the receiving line unless he is also the father of the groom.

—sits to the bride's right at a seated reception.

—proposes the first toast to the new couple for health, happiness, and prosperity.

—acts as the master of ceremonies, introducing any speakers, the cake-cutting ceremony, the tossing of the bouquet and garter, etc.

—mingles with guests.

—helps the groom into his going-away clothes at the end of the reception.

—checks that all luggage is in the car.

—leads the couple through the waiting guests to the exit and escorts them to their car.

—may drive them to the hotel or airport.

- After the reception, he

—promptly returns both his and the groom's rented formal wear to the appropriate location.

—may help in entertaining out-of-town guests.

Responsibilities of the Ushers

- Before the wedding, they

—pay for their own wedding attire, purchased or rented.

—are responsible for making and keeping appointments for fittings.

—try on formal attire before the wedding, preferably before leaving the store in case any sizes need to be exchanged.

—attend the rehearsal and rehearsal dinner.

- At the ceremony site, they

—arrive at the appointed time.

—assemble to the left of the entrance thirty to forty-five minutes before the ceremony begins.

—greet arrivals and encourage them to sign the guest book, and then be seated.

—usher as follows:

couple: take woman's arm, and man follows

family: take wife's arm; husband and family follow

two girls: take one on each arm

two women: escort the elder; the younger woman follows

men: simply accompany men to their seats unless they need assistance

Remain standing by the pew until the person is seated.

—when the guests do not present a pew card, ask if they are friends of the bride or groom.

—seat the guests accordingly: the bride's guests on the left, the groom's on the right. (In Jewish weddings, the seating is reversed.) In a military wedding, guests who are officers are seated according to rank.

—show late-arriving guests to seats on the side with more room.

- During the ceremony, they

—may participate in the processional (but often enter with the groom).

—generally escort the bridesmaids in the recessional.

- After the ceremony, they

—may return to usher out the guests.

—if asked, should be able to direct guests to restroom and phone facilities, and to the reception site.

—make certain the ceremony site is cleared of all the wedding party's belongings.

- At the reception, they

  —do not stand in the receiving line.

  —sit at either the bride's table or another table designated for the attendants, in alternating positions with the bridesmaids.

  —mingle with guests.

- After the reception, they

  —promptly return any rented formal wear to the appropriate location.

- Throughout the wedding and reception, they are to remain available to assist in whatever capacity asked by the best man or head usher.

Responsibilities of the Head Usher

(in addition to the previously stated responsibilities for the position of usher)

- The head usher is in charge of the other ushers.

- He assures their prompt arrival at the ceremony site for the rehearsal and wedding.

- When the ushers have not been designated by the bride and groom to perform special duties, the head usher appoints them at the rehearsal.

- He informs the ushers of any special seating arrangements.

- He makes certain the groom and the best man have received their boutonnieres.

- He supervises the seating, maintaining a balance of guests on both sides, particularly during the last fifteen minutes prior to the ceremony.

- He escorts the mothers of the bride and groom (unless another usher is the son of one of the mothers).

Responsibilities of the Ring Bearer

- Before the wedding, he

  —pays for his own attire, purchased or rented.

  —is responsible for making and keeping appointments for fittings.

  —tries on formal attire before the wedding, preferably before leaving the store in case any sizes need to be exchanged.

  —attends the rehearsal.

  —may attend the rehearsal dinner along with his parents.

- During the ceremony, he

  —carries a pillow that may or may not have the official rings attached.

  —either precedes or walks with the flower girl directly in front of you and your father in the processional.

  —may then, if very young, be seated with his parents.

  —if remaining with the bridal party, follows directly behind the bride and groom in the recessional along with the flower girl.

- At the reception, he

  —does not stand in the receiving line.

  —either remains with his parents or sits at a special table for children under adult supervision.

- After the reception, he

  —is responsible for promptly returning any rented formal wear to the appropriate location.

GROOM'S ATTENDANTS LIST

Best Man
Address _____ Phone _____
City _____ State _____ Zip _____
Sizes: Coat _____ Sleeve _____ Neck _____ Waist _____
      Inseam _____ Shoe _____ Height _____ Weight _____
Your Gift for Him _____

Head Usher
Address _____ Phone _____
City _____ State _____ Zip _____
Sizes: Coat _____ Sleeve _____ Neck _____ Waist _____
      Inseam _____ Shoe _____ Height _____ Weight _____
Your Gift for Him _____

Usher
Address _____ Phone _____
City _____ State _____ Zip _____
Sizes: Coat _____ Sleeve _____ Neck _____ Waist _____
      Inseam _____ Shoe _____ Height _____ Weight _____
Your Gift for Him _____

Usher
Address _____ Phone _____
City _____ State _____ Zip _____
Sizes: Coat _____ Sleeve _____ Neck _____ Waist _____
      Inseam _____ Shoe _____ Height _____ Weight _____
Your Gift for Him _____

Usher
Address _____ Phone _____
City _____ State _____ Zip _____
Sizes: Coat _____ Sleeve _____ Neck _____ Waist _____
      Inseam _____ Shoe _____ Height _____ Weight _____
Your Gift for Him _____

Usher

Address _____ Phone _____

City _____ State _____ Zip _____

Sizes: Coat _____ Sleeve _____ Neck _____ Waist _____

       Inseam _____ Shoe _____ Height _____ Weight _____

Your Gift for Him _____

Usher/Ring Bearer

Address _____ Phone _____

City _____ State _____ Zip _____

Sizes: Coat _____ Sleeve _____ Neck _____ Waist _____

       Inseam _____ Shoe _____ Height _____ Weight _____

Your Gift for Him _____

Groom's Attendants' Guidelines

(for the week before the wedding)

- Have final fittings for your wedding attire.
- Make sure you have everything you need—coat, trousers, shirt, vest, tie or ascot, cummerbund, shoes, socks, gloves, suspenders, studs, and cuff links.
- Gather all essentials ahead of time and place in one area to avoid last-minute frazzled nerves while trying to find something you've forgotten.
- Get plenty of rest.

BACHELOR PARTY
Location _____
Address _____
Date _____ Time _____ Phone _____

REHEARSAL AT CEREMONY SITE
Location _____
Address _____
Date _____ Time _____ Phone _____

REHEARSAL DINNER
Location _____
Address _____
Date _____ Time _____ Phone _____

ARRIVAL TIME AT THE WEDDING SITE FOR THE CEREMONY _____

WHERE TO DRESS _____

PHOTOGRAPHS
Location _____
Address _____
Date _____ Time _____ Phone _____

RECEPTION
Location _____
Address _____
Date _____ Time _____ Phone _____

TRANSPORTATION
To the ceremony site _____
To the reception site _____

OTHER _____

USHERS' ASSIGNMENTS

(Indicate ushers responsible for each item.)

1. Inform the groom of the bride's arrival at the ceremony site.

2. Candlelighting:

3. Seat and return:

   the groom's grandmother   row #_____   _____

   the bride's grandmother   row #_____   _____

   the groom's mother   row #_____   _____

   the bride's mother   row #_____   _____

4. Additional special seating:

   NAME   Row #

   _____   _____   _____

   _____   _____   _____

   _____   _____   _____

   _____   _____   _____

   _____   _____   _____

   _____   _____   _____

   _____   _____   _____

5. Draw and remove aisle ribbons (optional use). _____

   _____

6. Draw aisle runner (may already be in place). _____

   _____

7. Dismiss the remainder of guests. _____

   _____

8. Oversee the removal of any flowers to the reception site (especially when the reception is being held at another location). _____

   _____

9. Remove any apparel belonging to the bridal party after the ceremony. _____

   _____

10. Other assignments: _____

    _____

The Reception

The Reception
How-To

- The type of your reception should be compatible with the ceremony style. There are three general types of receptions:

  —A tea or stand-up buffet, for an early- or late-afternoon wedding, usually consists of hors d'oeuvres, wedding cake, and beverage, and allows approximately eight pieces of finger food in the per-person cost.

  —A sit-down buffet, for a morning, noon, or evening wedding, allows guests to serve themselves and then be seated at tables.

  —A sit-down dinner, for a wedding held after 6 P.M., offers a four- or five-course meal that is served to seated guests.

- The basic requirements for a reception are the wedding cake and a beverage for toasting the bridal couple.

- Champagne is traditionally served at formal receptions, but the serving of alcoholic beverages of any kind is a matter of choice.

- The reception is likely to consume the largest portion of your wedding budget.

- Appoint someone reliable to oversee the reception, using the Reception Organizer (pages 130–31) to answer questions, coordinate last-minute details, and direct cleanup.

- The Reception Organizer, Reception Seating Chart, Reception Receiving Line, Reception Room Diagrams, and worksheet for the table layout may be filled out, photocopied, and given to the reception coordinator.

Reception Site

- You will need to coordinate available dates and times with both the ceremony and reception sites before confirmation can be made.

- The selection of a reception site is largely determined by the size of your guest list.

- It is important to have a room that is neither too large nor too small.

—Your guests may feel lost in a room too large. To make the room appear smaller, you can partition off an area using potted plants, roping, or moveable room dividers.

—If a room is too small, it may become cramped and uncomfortable. When weather and location permit, the reception could spill over into a garden or patio to increase the size of the area.

• Allow approximately three hours for your reception. The length will depend upon the style of the reception, the location you have chosen, and the number of guests to be served.

• Most hotels and caterers, who may be involved with more than one reception on any given day, prefer that you select a time for your reception that stays within a single conventional time period: morning, noon, afternoon, or evening. If your reception extends into a second time period—such as from afternoon into evening—you may find difficulty in reserving a room, or an increase in cost for the use of the room and services.

• When you have a choice of using all or some of the services offered with a possible reception site (perhaps in a "package" deal), consider every detail before deciding. Packages may include (a) room, food, and service; or (b) room, food, service, cake, and decorations.

• Most hotels require that you use their food and beverage services. Hotels sometimes offer extras with their packages, such as discounted room prices for out-of-town guests, and special wedding night rates for the bride and groom.

• When reserving a reception room months in advance of your wedding, ask for a guaranteed price and get it in writing.

• Make certain that any contract you sign includes only those services you desire, including a cancellation policy whereby you get most of your money back should you cancel (particularly if the location is rebooked by another group).

• Some locations will allow you to reserve a room for a time before signing a contract; however, a deposit is required at signing—usually 10 percent of the total estimated cost.

Caterer

- If you are using a catering service, the time and date of your wedding must be confirmed with them and also with the ceremony and reception sites before you order any invitations.

- When seeking a caterer:

  —ask your family and friends for recommendations.

  —ask any unknown caterers for references, and samples of their food, if possible.

- By informing an experienced caterer of the amount you have budgeted for the event, the facilities to be used, and the number of invited people, he can quickly tell you what can be served, in what amount, and in what style.

- If the caterer is not familiar with the reception site you have selected, have him visit it to determine what is available and what is needed to make it functional for preparing and serving the food.

- Determine who is responsible for renting any needed extras—kitchen and serving equipment, tables, chairs, linens, table settings, etc.

- Most caterers break down the cost into a per-person charge.

- Ask if the quoted price also includes the tax and gratuity.

- You may want to ask who gets the leftover food (since you will have already paid for it).

- Ask how many people the caterer will provide for serving the food.

  —A buffet table requires a server for every main dish.

  —A sit-down dinner requires a server for every ten guests.

  —Beverages require a server for every fifty guests.

- Sometimes, even if you provide the cake, the beverages, and their respective servers, there is a service charge added by the caterer or reception site, especially when they offer the same service. This charge can be extra or hidden in the total per-person charge.

- When you sign a contract, be certain it specifies exactly what is to be served, the number of people serving it, the per-person cost, the payment schedule, and a release clause should you have to cancel.

Ordering Your Wedding Cake

- While seeking estimates for the wedding cake from the banquet manager, caterer, or bakery, taste samples to determine the quality of the cake they offer.

- You'll need an estimate of the number of guests you're expecting when you order your cake.

- Most prices are based on a per-serving cost. A down payment is usually required when ordering.

- The number of needed servings determines both the size and shape of the cake—the number of servings per layer size.

- Do not hesitate to inquire if, with their guidance, you can design your own cake.

- It's better to have the bakery deliver the cake to the reception site. They can then make any necessary repairs to the icing.

- Do not be afraid to ask friends to cut and serve the cake, even if they have never done it before. It isn't difficult when given proper instruction.

- To preserve the top layer of your cake, wrap it first in plastic wrap, then in two layers of aluminum foil before sealing with freezer tape.

- If you order more cake than you actually need, you may donate any uncut portions to nursing homes, charitable dining rooms, and others.

Cake Setup

- The wedding cake may be used as a centerpiece on the bride's table or on the buffet table, or it may be placed on its own table. When deciding on the best location, consider serving accessibility as well as how to best highlight the cake.

- Knowing the design of your cake—round, square, banquet, or heart-shaped—consider what table would best enhance its appearance.

- Cover the table with long cloths. Skirting may be necessary to cover the table to the floor.

- Trim the table and base of the cake with flowers, greenery, garlands, or bows. The bridesmaids' bouquets may also be placed on the table as part of the decorations.

Bridal Party Arrival

- Select someone other than a family member to serve as the unofficial reception host/hostess until the arrival of the bride's parents or other official hosts of the reception.

- Sometimes the bridal party can be detained due to completion of photographs at the ceremony site. For this reason, you may want to provide hors d'oeuvres and beverages for your guests preceding a buffet or sit-down dinner.

- The emcee, DJ, or bandleader can announce the arrival of the bridal party.

- You will want to provide the emcee with a list of names of those to be introduced. The list should be in order of their appearance. Include the phonetic pronunciation of each person's name as well as his or her relationship to you or the groom. Following is a suggested order of appearance:
    Bride's parents
    Groom's parents
    Bridesmaid and usher
    Bridesmaid and usher
    Bridesmaid and usher
    Bridesmaid and usher
    Maid/matron of honor and best man
    Bride and groom

Receiving Line

- Form the receiving line based on the best traffic flow for the room.

- The receiving line is for the bridal couple and their parents to greet guests and receive their congratulations. It should not disband until each guest in the line has been greeted.

- If you choose not to have a receiving line, you may circulate among the guests for the same purpose, greeting each one.

- Though sometimes held at the ceremony site, a receiving line is traditionally formed at the reception.

- You may greet any late arrivals as you mingle with your guests.

- To lessen the amount of time spent receiving guests, include only the bridal couple, parents, and honor attendants in the receiving line. Participants traditionally stand in this order: the bride's mother, the groom's mother, the bride, the groom, the maid of honor, and the bridesmaids (in order, with the bridesmaid who led the processional at the end of the line).

- If the fathers are included in the line, the groom's father stands next to the bride's mother and the bride's father stands between the bride and the groom's mother. (If the bride's father participates in the line, the best man assumes the role of reception host until the bride's father is free.)

- Take into consideration your family situation when deciding who will participate in the receiving line and where they will stand, particularly if your parents are divorced.

Guest Book

- Locate the guest book near the entrance or at the end of the receiving line.

- The book can be circulated among the guests to be sure everyone has signed it.

- The person (or persons) who tended the book at the ceremony site could also tend it at the reception (or others could be designated).

Seating Arrangements

- Tea or stand-up buffet:

  —You may have a bride's table and two or three other tables designated for the bridal party, parents, grandparents, and other family members.

—It's better to have only half as many chairs as guests, to allow room for people to move about.

—A few tables should be placed about the room to receive the empty plates, cups, and forks.

• Sit-down buffet or dinner:

—The bride's table generally includes the bride's and groom's attendants, other than children, sitting in alternating positions on either side of the bridal couple:

USHER / BRIDESMAID / USHER / BRIDESMAID / BEST MAN / BRIDE / GROOM / MAID OF HONOR / USHER / BRIDESMAID / USHER / BRIDESMAID

—Bridesmaids and ushers may be seated at specially designated tables other than the bride's table.

—The parents' table can have both sets of parents seated with the officiant and his or her spouse. You could also have separate tables for the bride's and groom's parents. Other honored guests can be seated with the parents with this arrangement:

BRIDE'S MOTHER

GROOM'S FATHER   WEDDING OFFICIANT

GRANDPARENT, FRIEND   GRANDPARENT, FRIEND

OFFICIANT'S WIFE   GROOM'S MOTHER

BRIDE'S FATHER

—When the bride's parents are divorced, the groom's parents sit with the parent who raised the bride. The other parent sits with his or her family and friends at a separate table.

—If there are children in the wedding party, they may either be seated with their parents or at a special children's table under adult supervision.

• If you are planning to have assigned seating, use the Reception Seating Chart to help you plan.

• If you use assigned seating, you may want to use the following method to help avoid confusion or traffic blocks among the guests: 1) conspicuously but tastefully display a number card on each table; 2) write each guest's name and assigned table number on a name/seating card; 3) place the cards on a hostess table near the entrance to the reception area so that guests can find their seats easily.

Cutting the Cake

- At a tea or stand-up buffet where the wedding cake is the main part of the menu, you may cut the cake before the receiving line forms.

- At a sit-down buffet you could hold the cake-cutting ceremony once all your guests have gone through the receiving line.

- At a full-course sit-down dinner, the cutting and sharing of the cake by the bridal couple comes just prior to the dessert course.

- Whenever you decide to cut your cake, consider how the timing affects your guests—too long a wait often results in a great deal of leftover cake.

- You and the groom are the first to cut the wedding cake. The groom places his right hand over yours on the knife handle as you together take a slice of cake from the bottom tier. The groom gives you the first bite, and you offer the groom the second.

- After sharing your first piece of cake, you and the groom may serve your respective new in-laws. Afterward, those serving the cake will serve the bridal attendants and remaining guests.

- It is nice to decorate the handle of the cake knife with flowers, bows, or streamers.

- In a military wedding, the bride and groom use his sword/saber to cut the first slice of cake.

Entertainment

- The following are a few of the more common wedding traditions:

  —*Toasting the bridal couple*: This usually begins right after the receiving line is completed, and before the food is served at a formal reception. It is traditionally led by the best man. Following a military wedding, the first toast usually welcomes the bride into the service. The arch may again be formed over her head during the toast.

—*First dance:* The bride and groom traditionally dance first, followed by these pairings:

    (a) bride and her father, groom and his mother

    (b) bride and the best man, groom and the maid of honor

    (c) bride and groom's father, groom and bride's mother

    (d) everyone joins in

It is not necessary for the bridal couple to dance the entire number before the father of the bride cuts in, or everyone is asked to join in.

When family relationships have been disrupted through divorce, the bride and groom may share their first dance together and then open the floor for everyone else.

At large formal affairs, dancing may begin at any time, even as early as the first arrival of guests to the reception. When dancing has begun early, a fanfare may be played to clear the floor and signal the bridal couple's first dance. The first dance may occur immediately following the toasts.

—*Throwing the bouquet and garter:* These popular customs come near the end of the reception just before the bride and groom change into their going-away clothes. The bride first tosses her bouquet over her shoulder to the waiting unmarried women, followed by the groom's removing the satin and lace garter from the bride's leg and then tossing it to the waiting single men. Florists will make up a special bouquet for throwing if you want to save your own. (These customs are generally not observed at a second wedding.)

—*Throwing the rice:* Designate younger sisters, cousins, or friends to distribute the rice, confetti, balloons, bubbles, or birdseed to guests. (Again, this custom is usually omitted at a second wedding.) Check with the ceremony/reception site on their policy regarding this tradition.

• Other forms of entertainment to consider:

—The best man or emcee could read congratulatory messages received during the day.

—Slides or a video montage of your individual childhoods and romance could be shown.

—Solos, poetry, and special readings written just for you are some of the ways your loved ones could share in your day.

—"Your song" could be sung or played by a group of friends, college pals, coworkers, etc.

—Speeches could be given by your families or close friends, offering their best wishes and perhaps sharing a few anecdotes from your past. Each should be kept to a minimum of time, no more than one or two minutes.

• Other local and ethnic customs may be observed; the following are a few examples:

—*The dollar dance:* Guests pay a dollar each to dance with the bride or groom. They may pin the money to the bride's gown or put money or checks into a small white satin purse the bride wears on her wrist.

—*The grand march:* Near the end of the reception, the emcee announces the grand march. The bride and groom lead the way, followed by their attendants and guests. As the music is played, the bridal couple leads the crowd around the room and sometimes even outside and around the building. At the end, everyone passes by the bridal couple so they can thank each guest for helping them celebrate their wedding day.

After the Reception

• After the reception, there is still work to be done—plan for it!

• The amount of work will largely depend on where the reception is held. There will be far less to do when the reception is held at a hotel than in a church, a hall, or at home.

• No matter how much or how little needs to be done, assign people to assist with each cleanup detail. Have plenty of help!

Home and/or Garden Reception

In addition to much of the preceding information, you must also consider the following when planning a reception at home.

- Although truly memorable, a home or garden reception is not necessarily less expensive than one held elsewhere, and may entail a great deal more work.

- In preparing for the event, you may find yourself involved in special cleaning, painting, and landscaping projects. Therefore, it may be expedient to hire outside professional services to ease the workload.

- If you are not having a caterer, set up a work schedule to plan and prepare the food in advance.

- Serve beverages in 4- or 6-ounce glasses.

- Provide two glasses of beverage per person per hour; this amount may be higher in hotter climates.

- Particularly with an at-home reception, you will need to study your kitchen and
    —list any equipment needed to facilitate the preparation and serving of the food and beverages.
    —check to see if you have adequate electrical outlets.
    —check to see if the electrical appliances are in good working condition. Do not be caught at the last minute with a fifty-cup coffee maker that doesn't work.

- Study the general flow of the house and garden as you plan the location of food and beverage tables, the bride's, attendants', and parents' tables, and seating for the guests.

- It may be necessary to remove some of the furniture from your home to allow more room for your guests.

- To avoid any last-minute frustration over where to place a dish on a serving table, prepare a layout of each table showing what dish goes where. Then, prior to the reception, place a slip of paper with the name of the dish at each location.

- At a home or garden reception, you will need additional people assisting you with details:
    —a crew to set up the area—tables, chairs, etc.
    —extra people to assist in the kitchen

—someone to pick up after the family when they leave for the wedding and before they return for the reception (if the wedding is also being held at home, they could assist in straightening the house just prior to the wedding)

—someone to stand at each door or entrance to the house and garden to welcome guests and direct them to the reception area

—someone very reliable—perhaps a close personal friend—to supervise the buffet table and keep it well stocked

—someone to assist with serving—passing trays of hors d'oeuvres, beverages, etc.

—others to remove empty plates and cups when guests have finished

—someone to keep powder rooms clean and stocked

—a crew to clean up the entire area and to remove all litter after the reception

- Plan well in advance where to park your guests' cars. It may be necessary to have them park elsewhere and to provide a shuttle service to your home.

- Parking attendants at your home may be needed. You may also want to consider hiring an off-duty police officer to direct traffic.

- You may need to consider an alternate location in case of undesirable weather (or be prepared with canopies, tents, fans, or heaters). Consider enclosing the following information with your invitations, giving an alternative location:

In case of rain the _____
will be held at _____.

Post-Reception Parties

- When all the planning of the past few months has come to fruition, the wedding and reception are over, and the bride and groom have left for their honeymoon—now what? If the festivities occurred early in the day, the bride's parents might consider inviting family members, the groom's parents, and special friends to join them in an informal gathering at home. Continuing the celebration in an intimate home atmosphere, rather than having it come to an abrupt end at the close of the reception, will help the parents to better adjust to the change of pace after the furious activity of the last few months.

- The festivities could extend over the next several days with swimming and boating trips, picnics, and trips to museums, plays, sporting events, etc.

RECEPTION SITE ESTIMATE

OPTION #1

Name _____

Address _____

Contact person _____

Phone _____

Open Dates
    and Times _____

Approximate number of guests _____

Appointment date and time
_____

Description of facilities:
    Rental fee _____

Food and/or beverage packages:
    Cost per person _____

Wedding Cake:
    Cost per serving _____

Services:
    ❏ Cost included
    ❏ Extra cost _____

Seating and Table Arrangements

Decorations

Entertainment

Equipment

Miscellaneous:
    Time allowed for reception_____
    Overtime cost _____
    Cancellation fee _____

Gratuities included ❏ Yes ❏ No

Sales tax included in per-person cost:
        ❏ Yes ❏ No

Estimated total cost _____

Required deposit _____

OPTION #2

Name _____

Address _____

Contact person _____

Phone _____

Open Dates
    and Times _____

Approximate number of guests _____

Appointment date and time
_____

Description of facilities:
    Rental fee _____

Food and/or beverage packages:
    Cost per person _____

Wedding Cake:
    Cost per serving _____

Services:
    ❏ Cost included
    ❏ Extra cost _____

Seating and Table Arrangements

Decorations

Entertainment

Equipment

Miscellaneous:
    Time allowed for reception_____
    Overtime cost _____
    Cancellation fee _____

Gratuities included ❏ Yes ❏ No

Sales tax included in per-person cost:
        ❏ Yes ❏ No

Estimated total cost _____

Required deposit _____

RECEPTION SITE CHOICE

Name _____

Address _____

Contact person _____ Phone _____

Confirmed date _____ Confirmed time period _____

Type of reception _____

Room(s) _____

Date contract signed _____

Deposit of $ _____ Due on _____ Date paid _____

Final head count due on _____

Number of guests (committed) _____

Cost per person _____

Subtotal: Number of guests x Cost per person _____

Sales tax _____

Total cost _____

Less deposit _____

Balance due _____

NOTES

CATERER ESTIMATE

OPTION #1

Name _____

Address _____

Contact person _____

Phone _____

Open Dates
  and Times _____

Approximate number of guests _____

Menu choices, food and/or
  beverage packages
  Cost per person _____

Wedding Cake
  Cost per serving _____

Description of services
  ❏ Cost included
  ❏ Extra cost _____

Decorations
  (color of linen, tableware, etc.)

Equipment needs

Gratuities included ❏ Yes ❏ No

Sales tax included in per-person cost
  ❏ Yes ❏ No

Estimated total cost _____

Required deposit _____

Cancellation fee _____

OPTION #2

Name _____

Address _____

Contact person _____

Phone _____

Open Dates
  and Times _____

Approximate number of guests _____

Menu choices, food and/or
  beverage packages
  Cost per person _____

Wedding Cake
  Cost per serving _____

Description of services
  ❏ Cost included
  ❏ Extra cost _____

Decorations
  (color of linen, tableware, etc.)

Equipment needs

Gratuities included ❏ Yes ❏ No

Sales tax included in per-person cost
  ❏ Yes ❏ No

Estimated total cost _____

Required deposit _____

Cancellation fee _____

CATERER CHOICE

Name _____

Address _____

Contact person _____ Phone _____

Confirmed date _____ Confirmed time period _____

Type of reception _____

Food and/or beverage package _____

Cake _____

Services _____

Date contract signed _____

Deposit of $ _____ Due on _____ Date paid_____

Final head count due on _____

Number of guests (committed) _____

Cost per person _____

Subtotal: Number of guests x Cost per person _____

Sales tax _____

Total cost _____

Less deposit _____

Balance due _____

Notes

RECEPTION FOOD AND BEVERAGES

Wedding Cake

_____

_____

Beverages

_____

_____

Hors d'oeuvres

_____

_____

Entrées

_____

_____

Salads and Side Dishes

_____

_____

Breads

_____

_____

Desserts

_____

_____

CAKE ESTIMATE

OPTION #1

Name _____

Address _____

Contact person _____

Phone _____

Open Dates
and Times _____

Approximate number of guests _____

Cake description
(size, shape, type and number of
servings, fillings, icing type, styles
and colors, and ornaments)

• Wedding cake

• Groom's cake

Cost per serving:
Wedding cake _____
Groom's cake _____

Equipment
(serving implements, and style and
number of tables):

Extra Costs:
Cake tier supports and bases

_____

Cutting and serving fee _____
Serving implements _____
Delivery and setup _____

Total cost _____

OPTION #2

Name _____

Address _____

Contact person _____

Phone _____

Open Dates
and Times _____

Approximate number of guests _____

Cake description
(size, shape, type and number of
servings, fillings, icing type, styles
and colors, and ornaments)

• Wedding cake

• Groom's cake

Cost per serving:
Wedding cake _____
Groom's cake _____

Equipment
(serving implements, and style and
number of tables):

Extra Costs:
Cake tier supports and bases

_____

Cutting and serving fee _____
Serving implements _____
Delivery and setup _____

Total cost _____

Cake choice: #_____ Date confirmed _____

Total cost _____ Deposit paid _____ Balance due _____ by _____
(Payment increments: $_____ due _____)

Appointment to design and order cake _____

DESIGN YOUR WEDDING CAKE

WEDDING CAKE

Size (# of servings, # of layers and sizes)

Shape (round, square, oblong, heart-shaped, flat, or graduated in tiers)

Type (white, chocolate, spice, carrot, fruit, etc.)

Filling (custard, fruit, icing)

Icing (type—buttercream, fondant, etc.; style—ornate or simple; color—white, chocolate, pastel)

Ornaments (bride and groom, swans, bells, doves, hearts, cupids, frosting or fresh flowers)

GROOM'S CAKE

Size

Shape

Type

Icing

How to serve (individual servings wrapped or boxed, or served along with the wedding cake)

Reception Seating Chart

Bride's Table

Type and size of table _____

Number of chairs _____

Raised dais ❑ Yes ❑ No

Order of seating (diagram or list)

Parents' Table(s)

Type and size of table _____

Number of chairs per table _____

Order of seating (diagram or list)

Attendants' Table

Type and size of table _____

Number of chairs per table _____

Order of seating (diagram or list)

Table # _____

Table # _____

Table # _____

Table # _____

Table # _____

Table # _____

Type and size of table _____

Number of chairs per table _____

Order of seating (diagram or list)

Table # _____   Table # _____

Table # _____   Table # _____

Table # _____   Table # _____

Reception Receiving Line
(diagram, showing each participant)

Groom's Father

    Bride's Mother

        Groom's Mother

            Bride's Father

                The Bride

                    The Groom

                        Maid of Honor

                            Bridesmaids

RECEPTION ROOM DIAGRAMS

Location of receiving line, guest book, entertainment area, and tables for gifts, cake, and food and beverages

Location of bride's table, attendants' table(s), parents' table(s), and guest tables

RECEPTION ORGANIZER

Reception site _____ Room _____

Contact person _____ Phone _____

Date _____ Time _____ Planned length _____

Reception coordinator _____ Phone _____

1. Rooms available for decorating:
   When _____ By whom _____

   (For decorations, see the diagram on pages 129, 158.)

2. Rental equipment to be delivered or picked up:
   When _____ By whom _____

3. Tables and chairs set up:
   When _____ By whom _____

   (For placement, see the room diagram on page 129.)

4. Cake delivered or picked up:
   When _____ By whom _____

   (For placement, see the room diagram on page 129.)

5. Flowers:
   Contact person _____ Phone _____
   Delivered from florist _____
   Flowers delivered from ceremony site _____
   When _____ By whom _____

6. Musicians:
   Contact person _____ Phone _____

   (See the Musicians' Needs Checklist on page 149.)

7. Food and beverages:
   Contact person _____ Phone _____

   (For placement, see the room diagram on page 129.)

8. Hostesses (also known as the House Party):
   Guest book _____
   Gifts _____
   Cake cutting and serving _____

Serving beverages _____

Distributing rice _____

9. Cleanup and storage:

Item	When	By Whom	Deliver To
Bride's Gown	_____	_____	_____
Leftover Wedding Cake	_____	_____	_____
_____	_____	_____	_____
_____	_____	_____	_____
_____	_____	_____	_____
_____	_____	_____	_____
_____	_____	_____	_____
_____	_____	_____	_____
_____	_____	_____	_____
_____	_____	_____	_____
_____	_____	_____	_____
_____	_____	_____	_____
_____	_____	_____	_____
_____	_____	_____	_____
_____	_____	_____	_____
_____	_____	_____	_____
_____	_____	_____	_____
_____	_____	_____	_____
_____	_____	_____	_____
_____	_____	_____	_____
_____	_____	_____	_____
_____	_____	_____	_____
_____	_____	_____	_____
_____	_____	_____	_____
_____	_____	_____	_____
_____	_____	_____	_____
_____	_____	_____	_____
_____	_____	_____	_____

TABLE LAYOUT FOR THE AT-HOME RECEPTION

(diagrams of table locations, and food and beverage placement)

Services

INVITATIONS
HOW-TO

- Order invitations only when you have confirmation from your wedding and reception sites.

- Note the time of the reception on the reception cards in the event of an extended lag in time between the wedding and reception beyond the normal transit time needed between sites.

- A broad range of prices is available among the different styles of invitations, but the price of comparable invitations varies little from store to store.

- Most stores require a 50 percent deposit when ordering, with the balance to be paid at delivery.

- It's wise to order about 5 percent more invitations than needed to cover any mistakes or forgotten people.

- At the time you order the invitations, have the correct form for the names of the persons giving the wedding, the full names of the bride and groom, and the time, date, and location of the ceremony.

—If the wedding is given by your mother and father:

Mr. and Mrs. James T. Smith
request the honor of your presence
at the marriage of their daughter
Mary Sue
to
Robert John Brown
(etc.)

—If the wedding is given by you and the groom:

Mary Sue Smith
and
Robert John Brown
request the honor of your presence
at their marriage
(etc.)

—If the wedding is given by your mother, and your father is deceased:

Mrs. James T. Smith
requests the honor of your presence
at the marriage of her daughter
Mary Sue
(etc.)

—If your mother has remarried, use her present husband's name:

Mr. and Mrs. John C. Howard
request the honor of your presence
at the marriage of her daughter
Mary Sue Smith
(etc.)

—If the wedding is given by your mother, and your parents are divorced, use your mother's maiden name plus your father's last name:

Mrs. Anne Miller Smith
requests the honor of your presence
at the marriage of her daughter
Mary Sue
(etc.)

—If the wedding is given by your father, and either your parents are divorced or your mother is deceased:

Mr. James T. Smith
requests the honor of your presence
at the marriage of his daughter
Mary Sue
(etc.)

—If your father has remarried:

Mr. and Mrs. James T. Smith
request the honor of your presence
at the marriage of his daughter
Mary Sue
(etc.)

—If the wedding is given by your divorced parents, and each has remarried:

Mr. and Mrs. James T. Smith
and
Mr. and Mrs. Scott M. Jones
request the honor of your presence
at the marriage of their daughter
Mary Sue Smith
(etc.)

• When deciding what style of wording to use, remember that "the honor of your presence" usually refers to a religious or formal service and "the pleasure of your company" usually refers to a civil or casual service.

• Consultants at specialty shops are available to help you with the wording.

• The only difference in wording between military and civilian weddings is in the use of service titles. These titles are used in the following manner:

—army, marine corps: rank of captain or higher

—navy: rank of commodore or higher

Their rank precedes their name, and the service designation follows on the next line under their name:

Captain Robert John Brown
United States Army

—For officers whose ranks are below those listed above, list their name on a single line, with the line below showing their rank and service designation:

Robert John Brown

Lieutenant, United States Navy

—For military personnel without rank, list their name on a single line, with the line below showing their service designation:

Robert John Brown

United States Marine Corps

A bride in the military may omit using her own rank and service designation on the invitations unless she plans to be married in her uniform.

- The addressing should be handwritten. Traditionally it is done in black ink, but the same color as the printing may also be used.

- The invitations will come with two sets of envelopes.

- When addressing outer envelopes:

  —all formal titles such as doctor, captain, and reverend are written out.

  —semiformal titles such as Ms., Mr., and Mrs. are abbreviated.

  —avenue, street, road, etc., are written out, as are the city and state.

- The wording on the inner envelope should include the titles and the last names only of the invited adults. If you wish to invite children under the age of eighteen, write their first names on a line below their parents' on the inner envelope. Older children in the family should receive their own invitations. The phrase "and family" instead of the children's names should never be used.

Mr. and Mrs. Johnson

John, Scott, Sarah, and Sue

- Once the invitations are addressed, place all the enclosures in the envelopes in this manner:

  —Place the reception card inside the invitation.

—Put the response card in its envelope, and place inside invitation.

—Place map, if used, inside invitation.

—Place tissue over printing on invitation to prevent smudging.

—Tuck the invitation, folded edge down, into the inner envelope.

—Place the inner envelope into the outer envelope so the writing on inner envelope faces flap.

- When purchasing stamps for mailing, have the invitation, including all enclosures, weighed to determine the correct postage.

- Mail all the invitations at the same time, using first-class stamps.

- A stamp must be provided on the return envelope if response cards are used.

- The following example of response card wording eliminates confusion for your guests and increases the likelihood that they'll return the cards on time.

The favor of a reply
is requested before
June first.

*M*_____
will _____ *will not* _____ *attend.*

Number of persons: _____

- When ordering invitations, also order any other stationery accessories you may need.

—reception cards, showing the time and place of the event.

—response cards with printed reply-address envelopes, to be enclosed with the invitation so you can plan for the number of guests that will attend the reception.

—informal thank-you notes, having the name of the bride or the bride and groom on the outside, and blank on the inside.

—thank-you notes, with a preprinted message to acknowledge when a gift is received.

—personalized napkins and matches, for the guests to use or to keep as souvenirs.

—announcements, to be sent to those you would have liked to attend your wedding, but who couldn't.

—pew cards, rarely used, but appropriate for ultraformal wedding situations, e.g., with celebrities and dignitaries; the cards may be enclosed with the invitation or sent after the acceptance has been received to ensure the correct number of seats.

—wedding programs, showing the order of the service and listing all participants. These can be folded or rolled like a scroll and tied with ribbon. Not only does a printed program serve as a guide to your wedding ceremony, but it's also a keepsake for your guests.

   Programs can be engraved, printed with offset printing, or produced by word processor on a laser printer, with calligraphy added later.

   The program covers may be obtained from printers who offer a variety of paper stocks, from manufacturers of wedding invitations who offer several different styles, or from religious supply houses or bookstores who carry appropriate church bulletin covers. Or they can be of your own creation, including a photograph of the bridal couple, special drawings, etc.

   The program could contain the wedding date, time, and location; the names of all the participants, their positions in the wedding, and their relationship to the bride and groom; and the order of the ceremony, with any special readings or observances. Expressions of gratitude from the bridal couple to their families and guests, and any clarifying information regarding the wedding service or reception, could also be included.

   If possible, have your programs printed only two weeks or so before the wedding, to include any last-minute changes. Allow enough time, however, for proofreading the copy, making any corrections, and receiving delivery of the finished product.

• Thank-you notes do not have to be long, but they should be personal. To achieve this goal:

—mention your spouse's name.

—mention the gift.

—tell what you liked about the gift.

—tell how you will use it.

- It's better to use the blank thank-you notes (informals) rather than the preprinted ones.

- Thank-you notes that denote the couple as being married—Mr. and Mrs. Robert Brown, or Mary Sue and Robert Brown—should be reserved for use after the wedding. For notes sent before the wedding, the printing should read as in these examples: Mary Sue Smith and Robert Brown, or Mary Sue and Robert, or Mary Sue Smith.

- If the engagement is broken after the wedding invitations are in the mail and there is sufficient time, you may send a printed announcement of the change of plans, as in this example:

> *Mr. and Mrs. _____*
> *announce that the marriage of their daughter,*
> *_____ to Mr. _____,*
> *will not take place.*

When there isn't enough time, you'll need to phone each invited guest. It isn't necessary to reveal reasons for the breakup. Any gifts must be returned to the sender.

STATIONERY ESTIMATE

Option #1

Name _____
Contact person _____
Phone _____
Address _____

INVITATIONS—
 Style # _____ Print # _____
 Book _____
 Number needed _____
  Cost_____

RECEPTION CARDS—
 Style # _____ Print # _____
 Book _____
 Number needed _____
  Cost_____

RESPONSE CARDS—
 Style # _____ Print # _____
 Book _____
 Number needed _____
  Cost_____

THANK-YOU NOTES—
 Style # _____ Print # _____
 Book _____
 Number needed _____
  Cost_____

ANNOUNCEMENTS—
 Style # _____ Print # _____
 Book _____
 Number needed _____
  Cost_____

NAPKINS—
 Style # _____ Print # _____
 Book _____
 Number needed _____
  Cost_____

PROGRAMS—
 Style # _____ Print # _____
 Book _____
 Number needed _____
  Cost_____
  Total Cost _____

Option #2

Name _____
Contact person _____
Phone _____
Address _____

INVITATIONS—
 Style # _____ Print # _____
 Book _____
 Number needed _____
  Cost_____

RECEPTION CARDS—
 Style # _____ Print # _____
 Book _____
 Number needed _____
  Cost_____

RESPONSE CARDS—
 Style # _____ Print # _____
 Book _____
 Number needed _____
  Cost_____

THANK-YOU NOTES—
 Style # _____ Print # _____
 Book _____
 Number needed _____
  Cost_____

ANNOUNCEMENTS—
 Style # _____ Print # _____
 Book _____
 Number needed _____
  Cost_____

NAPKINS—
 Style # _____ Print # _____
 Book _____
 Number needed _____
  Cost_____

PROGRAMS—
 Style # _____ Print # _____
 Book _____
 Number needed _____
  Cost_____
  Total Cost _____

Stationery choice #_____ Date confirmed_____
Total Cost _____ Deposit paid _____ Balance due _____ by _____

STATIONERY WORDING

ITEM AND LINE NUMBERS

Invitation

1. _____
2. _____
3. _____
4. _____
5. _____
6. _____
7. _____
8. _____
9. _____
10. _____
11. _____
12. _____
13. _____
14. _____
15. _____
16. _____
17. _____
18. _____

Return Address for Envelope Flap

1. _____
2. _____
3. _____

Reception Cards

1. _____
2. _____
3. _____
4. _____

Response Cards

1. _____
2. _____
3. _____
4. _____

Response Address

1. _____
2. _____
3. _____

Thank-You Notes

1. _____
2. _____

Napkins

1. _____
2. _____

Announcements

1. _____
2. _____
3. _____
4. _____
5. _____
6. _____
7. _____
8. _____
9. _____
10. _____

Notes

_____
_____
_____

PROGRAM WORDING

_____
_____
_____
_____
_____
_____
_____
_____
_____
_____
_____
_____
_____
_____
_____
_____
_____
_____
_____
_____
_____
_____
_____
_____
_____
_____
_____
_____
_____
_____
_____
_____
_____
_____

MUSIC HOW-TO

- The Musicians' Guidelines may be filled out, photocopied, and given to the ceremony and reception musicians in advance of your wedding day.

Ceremony

- The music should be in keeping with the style of wedding you have chosen—formal, semiformal, or informal. This is achieved through the use of traditional, sacred, and contemporary music, combining one or more types of music for a pleasing effect (see the Musical Selection Ideas on page 147).

- If you are being married in a church, the church organist can offer many suggestions of appropriate wedding music and acquaint you with any possible restrictions on the type of music that may be used.

- You may elect to use only one selection of music for the entire processional or choose to have one for the entrance of the other members of the bridal party and another for yourself.

- When only one selection is used for the processional, the instrumentalist(s) may increase the volume of the music to indicate your entrance.

- When a separate selection is being used for your processional, the organist could chime the hour, play a fanfare, or add a flourish of trumpets or chimes to signal your entrance.

- Each selection of music may be played a little faster or slower, a little louder or softer. By changing the pace and the level of sound, a selection may be appropriate for use as either a processional (slower) or a recessional (faster).

- When using more than one instrumentalist for the processional (i.e., duet, trio, quartet, or quintet), it is recommended that you ask them to attend the rehearsal to practice the timing of the entrance of the entire bridal party.

- Find out also whether the church requires you to use only their own musicians before you ask someone else to participate.

- Your choice of instrumentalists and vocalists may be restricted by the ceremony site.

- Be sure you have heard the individuals perform before asking them to be part of your wedding day.

- Be prepared to pay each musician either a fee set by the individual or union scale.

- Give them a payment envelope at the close of the wedding rehearsal, if they attend, or upon arrival the day of the wedding.

- If the performers need any special music, you are responsible for getting it to them as soon as possible.

- They will need time to work any necessary rehearsals into their schedules.

- Have the musicians be responsible for setting their own practice times, dates, and locations with each other. You might check later to see if they are prepared.

Reception

- Use the same procedure in hiring musicians for the reception as you do for the wedding. You might consider using the same musicians for both.

- Especially with groups, be sure you're hiring the musicians you're hearing.

- Use a combination of musical styles to entertain your guests—classical, Broadway tunes, pop, rock, or ethnic.

- To provide continuous music, you may use a combination of live and taped music.

- You may decide to have only recorded music. A professional disc jockey is usually an experienced emcee and is able to entertain your guests with a variety of music styles.

- Be sure to set a limit on the level of sound for any amplified instruments. The sound level should not hinder conversation.

- Payment to the musicians should be made immediately before they leave the reception area.

- You might consider inviting your guests to have a special part in your day by sharing their talents during the reception.

MUSICAL SELECTION IDEAS

Bach
Adagio Cantabile [1]
Andante from *Brandenburg Concerto No. 2* [2]
Arioso in A [1, 2]
"Jesu, Joy of Man's Desiring" [2, 3]
"Sheep May Safely Graze" [1]

Bach, Gounod
"Ave Maria" [4]

Beethoven
"Joyful, Joyful, We Adore Thee" [2, 3, 5]

Berlioz
Trio for Two Flutes and Harp from *L'Enfance du Christ* [1]

Bliss
Wedding Fanfare and March [2]

Bradbury
"Savior, Like a Shepherd Lead Us" [4]

Brown
"This Is the Day" (or, "A Wedding Song") [3]

Campra
"Riguadon" [2, 5]

Clarke
Trumpet Voluntary: Prince of Denmark's March [2, 5]

Copland
"Bridal Prayer" [3]

Cutting, Anonymous
"Greensleeves" [4]

Diggle
Wedding Prelude [1]

Gounod
"Entreat Me Not to Leave Thee" [3, 4]

Grieg
"I Love Thee" [3]

Handel
Largo [2]
Allegro Maestoso ("The Horn Pipe") from *Water Music Suite* [2, 5]
Sonata for Bells [2]

Hustad
"Love That Wilt Not Let Me Go" [3]

Johnson, D.
"Keep Us One" [3]
Trumpet Tune in D [2, 5]

Karg, Elert
"Now Thank We All Our God" [5]

Lamb, Rosasco
"Household of Faith" [3]

Lemmons
Fanfare [2, 5]

Liszt
"Liebestraum" [1]

Malotte
"The Lord's Prayer" [3, 4]

Marcello
"Psalm 19" [5]

Mendelssohn
"On Wings of Song" [1]
Wedding March from *A Midsummer Night's Dream* [5]

Mouret
Rondeau [1]

Pachelbel
Canon in D [2]

Peterson
"Jesus, Guest at Cana's Wedding" [3]

Purcell
Trumpet Tune and Air [2, 5]

Purifoy
"Here We Are Now" [3]

Rodgers, Hammerstein
Wedding processional from *The Sound of Music* [2]

Schreiner
"A Wedding March" [2]

Schumann
"Thou Art Like a Flower" [3, 4]

Scott, Coomes, North
"Our Love" [3]

Sheppard
"Me and My House" [3]

Stanley
Trumpet Voluntary [2]

Vangelis
Five Circles Theme from *Chariots of Fire* [2]

Wagner
Bridal Chorus ("Here Comes the Bride") from *Lohengrin* [2]

Walton, W.
The Crown Imperial March [5]

Widor
Toccata from Symphony No. 5 [5]

Williams
"A Wedding Prayer" [3]

Young, G.
Prelude in Classic Style [1, 2, 5]

MUSIC ESTIMATE

Music needed for: ❑ Ceremony only ❑ Reception only ❑ Both

Hours needed: Ceremony _____ Reception _____

Contact/agent _____ Phone _____
Address _____
Rate per hour _____ Overtime rate _____
Rest breaks: How many _____ How often _____
Audition date _____ Time _____ Place _____
Notes: _____

Choice: ❑ Yes ❑ No

Contact/agent _____ Phone _____
Address _____
Rate per hour _____ Overtime rate _____
Rest breaks: How many _____ How often _____
Audition date _____ Time _____ Place _____
Notes: _____

Choice: ❑ Yes ❑ No

Contact/agent _____ Phone _____
Address _____
Rate per hour _____ Overtime rate _____
Rest breaks: How many _____ How often _____
Audition date _____ Time _____ Place _____
Notes: _____

Choice: ❑ Yes ❑ No

MUSICIANS' NEEDS
CHECKLIST

Musicians' needs for: ❏ Ceremony only ❏ Reception only ❏ Both

NEEDS	YES	NO	NUMBER
Piano tuned	❏	❏	_____
Folders	❏	❏	_____
Music stands	❏	❏	_____
Seating	❏	❏	_____
Electrical outlets	❏	❏	_____

Sound Equipment

Microphones	❏	❏	_____
placement _____			
Amplifiers	❏	❏	_____
placement _____			

Sound Operator

Name _____

Address _____

Organ ❏ ❏ _____

Placement _____

Piano ❏ ❏ _____

Placement _____

Storage for Instruments ❏ ❏ _____

Location _____

Dressing Area ❏ ❏ _____

Location _____

If ceremony or reception is being held outdoors:

Is there a shady spot for musicians? ❏ ❏ _____

Where would they go if it rains? _____

CEREMONY MUSIC

Wedding site _____

Contact person _____ Phone _____

Appointment date _____ Time _____ Place _____

INSTRUMENTALIST	PHONE
_____	_____
_____	_____
_____	_____
_____	_____
_____	_____

SOLOIST	PHONE
_____	_____
_____	_____
_____	_____

CEREMONY ORDER	SELECTION	MUSICIAN
Prelude	_____	_____
	_____	_____
	_____	_____
Processional	_____	_____
	_____	_____
	_____	_____
Recessional	_____	_____
	_____	_____
	_____	_____
Postlude	_____	_____
	_____	_____
	_____	_____

MUSICIANS' GUIDELINES—
CEREMONY

Wedding of _____

Ceremony site and address _____

Contact person _____ Phone _____

Wedding date _____ Arrival time _____

What to wear _____

INSTRUMENTALIST	PHONE
_____	_____
_____	_____
_____	_____
_____	_____
_____	_____

SOLOIST	PHONE
_____	_____
_____	_____

REHEARSALS	DATE	TIME	LOCATION
Special	_____	_____	_____
Special	_____	_____	_____
Wedding	_____	_____	_____

CEREMONY ORDER	SELECTION	MUSICIAN
Prelude	_____	_____
_____	_____	_____
_____	_____	_____
Processional	_____	_____
_____	_____	_____
_____	_____	_____
Recessional	_____	_____
_____	_____	_____
_____	_____	_____
Postlude	_____	_____
_____	_____	_____

RECEPTION MUSIC

Reception site _____

Contact person _____ Phone _____

Appointment date _____ Time _____ Place _____

General Music Selection—Possible Choices

LIVE

RECORDED

Special Music—Possible Choices

FANFARES

Arrival of the bridal couple _____

_____

Cutting of the cake _____

_____

Toast to the bridal couple _____

_____

Throwing of bouquet and garter _____

_____

FIRST DANCE

_____

_____

ETHNIC SELECTIONS

_____

_____

OTHER

_____

_____

Musicians' Guidelines— Reception

Wedding Reception of _____

Reception site and address _____

Contact person _____ Phone _____

Date _____ Arrival time _____

What to wear _____

Instrumentalists	Phone
_____	_____
_____	_____
_____	_____
_____	_____
_____	_____

Soloists	Phone
_____	_____
_____	_____

Program Order	Selection	Musician
_____	_____	_____
_____	_____	_____
_____	_____	_____
_____	_____	_____
_____	_____	_____
_____	_____	_____
_____	_____	_____
_____	_____	_____
_____	_____	_____
_____	_____	_____
_____	_____	_____
_____	_____	_____
_____	_____	_____
_____	_____	_____
_____	_____	_____

Sound level to be maintained: _____

Flowers How-To

- The Florist's Guidelines may be filled out, photocopied, and given to your florist in advance of your wedding day.

- When you visit the florist of your choice, have the following information: your wedding style, your wedding gown color and style, your bridal attendants' colored fabric swatches, the colors of the mothers' and grandmothers' dresses and what type of corsage they prefer (pinned to the shoulder, waist, or purse, or carried or worn on the wrist), pictures or diagrams of the ceremony and reception sites and their color schemes, any restrictions concerning the floral decorations or use of candles, an approximate number and types of arrangements you will need, and the length of the aisle you'll be using.

- Does the florist offer a wedding package? What is included? Can you make any substitutions?

- A skilled florist can stay within your floral budget by selecting flowers that are in season, by controlling the sizes of bouquets and corsages, by interspersing more greenery with the flowers, and by utilizing many of the flowers from the ceremony at the reception site.

- You might consider renting potted plants, flowers, and trees for decorations.

- The bridal bouquet may be very colorful or done entirely with white flowers and greenery using a combination of flowers in a variety of sizes. The style of the bouquet should complement the style of the gown:

  —formal gowns: cascade, crescent, or over-arm bouquets.

  —informal gowns: nosegay and oval-shaped bouquets or a few flowers wrapped with ribbon.

    The style of the bouquet should also complement the bride's height—smaller bouquets using more delicate flowers for petite brides, longer and larger bouquets for taller brides.

- Flowers to consider for your wedding are asters, camellias, daisies, freesia, gardenias, irises, lilies, lilies of the valley, orchids, roses, stephanotis, tulips, violets, and others.

- Flower arrangements (bouquets or centerpieces) may be made with silk or dried flowers, as well as fresh.

- If you decide to have a going-away corsage, it can be made as part of your bridal bouquet. The florists call this a "break-away bouquet."

- Have the florist make a small bouquet for tossing at the reception, particularly if you want to preserve your bridal bouquet.

- To identify the honor attendant, her bouquet can be a different color or larger than the other attendants'.

- The flower girl can carry petals or flowers in a basket or a miniature bouquet.

- The groom's boutonniere is usually taken from the flowers in the bride's bouquet and is different from all the other boutonnieres.

- Extra corsages and boutonnieres could be provided for the soloists, instrumentalists, officiant—if he isn't wearing a robe, guest book and gift attendants, wedding hostess, cake server and hospitality committee, and any other special people. Flowers are not necessary for those who charge a fee.

- Have the florist pin the individual names to the corsages, bouquets, and boutonnieres for easy dispersal at the ceremony site. To aid your wedding coordinator, have a family member or close friend available to identify those people other than the bridal party who are to receive flowers at your wedding.

- Keep the flowers refrigerated until the last possible moment.

- The individual bouquets may be inserted into water-filled tubes. Remove the bouquets and pat them dry before carrying.

- If you're not using spring-loaded candles, freeze the candles ahead of time to prevent or lessen their dripping. Then prelight them to ensure easy lighting during the ceremony.

- Don't use spring-loaded candles in the unity candelabra.

- If the aisle runner is to extend up the altar steps, be certain it's firmly secured to prevent slippage.

- The decorations for a military wedding may include the American flag and the colors of the bride's and/or groom's military units. Consult with the ceremony site for permission to use these.

- Boutonnieres are not worn with military uniforms.

- It's best at large weddings to have a guest book that can have its pages easily removed. By placing the pages on opposite ends of the table, you create two areas for signing. A floral table spray placed in the middle of the table could be used for decoration.

- If you are having only one place for your guests to register, then a small arrangement—perhaps two or three flowers, baby's breath, greenery, and a bow—could be used for the guest book stand.

- Stanchions placed outdoors and decorated with bows and greenery could be used to direct those guests unfamiliar with either the ceremony or reception sites.

- If your reception is a stand-up affair, only a few arrangements and garlands for the serving, punch, and cake tables will be needed.

- If the reception is a sit-down dinner, you will need to plan centerpieces for each table in addition to any other decoration you might desire.

- The bridal attendants' bouquets can be used as decorations by placing them around the cake or on the bride's table.

- To fully utilize your flowers, designate someone to transfer them from the ceremony site to the reception.

- The floral baskets from your ceremony could be positioned at either end of the receiving line, beside the cake table, or behind the bride's table.

- Any floral pew arrangements could also be used as decorations at the reception. Have the florist fix them for easy transfer.

- It's nice to order flowers to be sent to your parents' homes one or two days after the wedding as a special thank-you gift.

- Another nice gesture is to send flowers to your bridal shower and party hostesses. Tell the florist the kind, date, time, and place of each event.

FLORIST ESTIMATE

OPTION #1

Name _____

Address _____

Contact person _____

Phone _____

Appointment date and time:

_____

Wedding package

Cost _____

Description _____

OPTION #2

Name _____

Address _____

Contact person _____

Phone _____

Appointment date and time:

_____

Wedding package

Cost _____

Description _____

INDIVIDUAL CHOICES

	COST	
	OPTION #1	OPTION #2
Altar flowers—1st choice _____	$ _____	$ _____
2nd choice _____	_____	_____
Bride's bouquet—1st choice _____	_____	_____
2nd choice _____	_____	_____
Bridesmaids' bouquets—1st choice _____	_____	_____
2nd choice _____	_____	_____
Boutonnieres—1st choice _____	_____	_____
2nd choice _____	_____	_____
Corsages—1st choice _____	_____	_____
2nd choice _____	_____	_____

ACCESSORIES

	OPTION #1	OPTION #2
arch/canopy	$ _____	$ _____
kneeler	_____	_____
candelabra	_____	_____
candlelighters	_____	_____
candles	_____	_____
aisle runner	_____	_____
Other _____	_____	_____

SERVICES

	OPTION #1	OPTION #2
delivery	$ _____	$ _____
setup	_____	_____
removal	_____	_____
Other		
_____	_____	_____
_____	_____	_____

Choice # _____   Date confirmed _____

Total cost _____   Deposit paid _____   Balance due _____ by _____

FLORAL DIAGRAMS
(for the placement of flowers, plants, and other decorations)

Entry Area
(Including guest book stand
or table, and gift table)

Aisle and Altar

Reception Site

FLORAL PLANNING

Florist _____

Address _____

Contact person _____ Phone _____

Date _____ Time _____

Ceremony site and address _____

Contact person _____ Phone _____

Date _____ Time _____

Reception site and address _____

Contact person _____ Phone _____

Date _____ Time _____

Ceremony Flowers

QUANTITY	DESCRIPTION (COLOR, SIZE, VARIETY)	COST

BRIDE

_____ Bouquet _____ _____

_____ Small bouquet for throwing _____ _____

_____ Going-away corsage _____ _____

BRIDAL ATTENDANTS

_____ Honor attendant's bouquet _____ _____

_____ Bridesmaids' bouquets _____ _____

_____ Flower girl's bouquet _____ _____

_____ Floral headdresses _____ _____

GROOM AND ATTENDANTS

_____ Groom's boutonniere _____ _____

_____ Best man's boutonniere _____ _____

_____ Groomsmen/ushers' boutonnieres _____ _____

_____ Ring bearer's boutonniere _____ _____

MOTHERS AND GRANDMOTHERS

_____ Mother of the bride's corsage _____ _____

_____ Mother of the groom's corsage _____ _____

_____ Mothers' roses _____ _____

_____ Grandmothers' corsages _____ _____

_____ Corsages for other female family members
(such as stepmothers, foster mothers)

_____ _____ _____

_____ _____ _____

FATHERS AND GRANDFATHERS

_____ Father of the bride's boutonniere _____ _____

_____ Father of the groom's boutonniere _____ _____

_____ Grandfathers' boutonnieres _____ _____

_____ Boutonnieres for other male family members

(such as stepfathers, foster fathers)

_____ _____ _____

_____ _____ _____

ALTAR

_____ Arch/canopy _____ _____

_____ Kneeling bench _____ _____

_____ Candelabra _____ _____

_____ 3 candles, standing _____ _____

_____ 3 candles, tabletop unity _____ _____

_____ 7 candles, standing _____ _____

_____ 9 or 15 candles, fan, standing _____ _____

_____ 9 or 15 candles, spiral, standing _____ _____

_____ Candlelighters _____ _____

_____ White candles _____ _____

_____ Floral sprays _____ _____

_____ Beauty vases _____ _____

_____ Potted flowers _____ _____

_____ Potted plants _____ _____

_____ Potted trees _____ _____

_____ Plant stands _____ _____

_____ Other _____ _____

AISLE

_____ Pew decorations _____ _____

_____ Candelabra _____ _____

_____ Floral arrangements _____ _____

_____ Greenery and bows _____ _____

_____ Aisle ribbons _____ _____

_____ Aisle runner (length ____) _____ _____

_____ Other _____ _____

OTHERS FOR WHOM YOU MAY WISH TO PROVIDE FLOWERS

_____ Soloist(s) _____ _____

_____ Instrumentalist(s) _____ _____

_____ Officiant _____ _____

_____ Guest book attendant(s) _____ _____

_____ Gift attendant(s) _____ _____

_____ Wedding hostess/coordinator(s) _____ _____

_____ Cake servers _____ _____

_____ Hospitality committee _____ _____

_____ Others _____ _____

Reception Flowers

QUANTITY	DESCRIPTION (COLOR, SIZE, VARIETY)	COST

TABLE CENTERPIECES

_____ Bride's table _____ _____

_____ Parents' table _____ _____

_____ Attendants' table(s) _____ _____

_____ Guest tables _____ _____

_____ Other _____ _____

OTHER DECORATIONS

_____ Table garlands _____ _____

_____ Cake _____ _____

_____ Receiving line area _____ _____

_____ Guest book stand _____ _____

_____ Table for receiving gifts _____ _____

_____ Ladies' powder room _____ _____

_____ Other _____ _____

Service Costs

Delivery $_____

Setup $_____

Removal $_____

Other _____ $_____

Delivery $_____

Setup $_____

Removal $_____

Other _____ $_____

FLORIST'S GUIDELINES

Wedding of _____

Address _____

Phone _____

Ceremony site _____

Address _____

Contact person _____ Phone _____

Date _____ Delivery/Setup time _____

Removal time _____

Reception site _____

Address _____

Contact person _____ Phone _____

Date _____ Delivery/Setup time _____

Removal time _____

NOTES

PHOTOGRAPHY HOW-TO

- The Photographer's Planning List and Guidelines may be filled out, photocopied, and given to your photographer in advance of your wedding day.

- To ensure good-quality pictures, it's best to employ a professional photographer.

- When you're selecting a photographer, study his portfolio; ask if the same person who shot the pictures you're examining will be the one to shoot your wedding; and ask about any package plans he offers.

- The cost of the different packages is controlled by adjusting the quality and sizes of prints, the size of the album, and any extra services. These vary from one photographer to another, so be sure you understand exactly what is being offered.

- When you have decided on a photographer, discuss any restrictions to be observed during the ceremony, concerning such details as flashbulbs and the photographer's being at the altar or otherwise visible to guests.

- When planning your formal bridal portrait one to two months in advance, have your hair styled and makeup applied the same as it will be on your wedding day.

- More and more couples are having their formal pictures taken—including the bridal portrait—at the ceremony site before the service. It is a tradition, but one based on superstition, that prevents the bride and groom from seeing each other on their wedding day before the ceremony.

- By having your portrait taken on your wedding day

    —you avoid having to transport your gown to a studio and back, running the risk of soiling it.

    —you will have your own wedding bouquet in the picture.

    —you will be photographed at your best—a glowing bride.

- To take the pictures before the wedding, you, your groom, your attendants, and families will need to be at the ceremony site approximately three hours before the wedding, allowing thirty to forty-five minutes to dress, up to two hours for photographs, and thirty to forty-five minutes to prepare for the arrival of the wedding guests.

- By taking all the formal pictures before the wedding, the groom will not have that special moment of first seeing you as you come down the aisle. Therefore, arrange a time for the two of you to be alone immediately before having your pictures taken. This could also be a special time spent with both sets of parents or with your maid of honor and best man. Be creative with this time—the sharing of special music, poetry, Scripture, or prayer.

- If you want to wait until the ceremony for the groom to see you, then schedule only the taking of the separate formals and individual family pictures just prior to the ceremony time. Out of consideration for your guests, set a time limit for finishing the formal pictures after the ceremony.

- You may want to designate a close friend or family member to assist the photographer at the reception by identifying other special people to be photographed.

- Be aware that viewing your proofs can be an emotion-packed time. Undoubtedly you will need to eliminate some great pictures to maintain your budget.

PHOTOGRAPHER'S ESTIMATE

OPTION #1	OPTION #2
Photographer _____	Photographer _____
Address _____	Address _____
Contact person _____	Contact person _____
Phone _____	Phone _____
Appointment date and time:	Appointment date and time:
_____	_____

DESCRIPTION OF WEDDING PACKAGES
(including cost and required deposit) — both columns
_____
_____
_____
_____
_____

INDIVIDUAL PORTRAITS (both columns)

Bridal portrait
(part of package ❑ extra ❑)
Cost _____ Deposit _____

Engagement photos
(part of package ❑ extra ❑)
Cost _____ Deposit _____

Glossies for newspaper
(part of package ❑ extra ❑)
Cost _____ Deposit _____

Additional copies
(part of package ❑ extra ❑)
Cost _____ Deposit _____

Other
(part of package ❑ extra ❑)
Cost _____ Deposit _____

Photographer choice #_____ Date confirmed _____
Total cost _____ Deposit paid _____ Balance due _____ by _____
Payment: Credit card ❑ Cash only ❑ Date to view proofs _____

PHOTOGRAPHER'S PLANNING
LIST AND GUIDELINES

Bride's name _____ Phone _____

Address _____

Wedding: Date _____ Time _____

    Place _____ Room # _____

Reception: Date _____ Time _____

    Place _____ Room # _____

Engagement pictures:

Time _____ Date _____ Place _____

Formal bridal portrait:

Time _____ Date _____ Place _____

Guidelines/ceremony site restrictions _____

_____

_____

What to wear _____

Other guidelines _____

Suggested formal shots:

BRIDE	GROOM	BRIDE AND GROOM
_____ alone	_____ alone	_____ together
with:	with:	with:
_____ father	_____ father	_____ best man
_____ mother	_____ mother	_____ maid of honor
_____ parents	_____ parents	_____ honor attendants
_____ maid of honor	_____ best man	_____ bridesmaids
_____ bridesmaids	_____ ushers	_____ ushers
_____ flower girl	_____ ring bearer	_____ flower girl & ring bearer
_____ grandparents	_____ grandparents	_____ grandparents
_____ family	_____ family	_____ both families
_____ _____	_____ _____	_____ bridal party
_____ _____	_____ _____	_____ bride's parents
_____ _____	_____ _____	_____ groom's parents
_____ _____	_____ _____	_____ officiant

Suggested shots at the reception:

_____ arrival	_____ food table	_____ reception line
_____ cutting the cake	_____ the toast	_____ bride throwing bouquet
_____ cake table	_____ bride table	_____ bride and groom
		_____ feeding each other cake
_____ _____	_____ _____	_____ _____
_____ _____	_____ _____	_____ _____

VIDEOTAPING AND AUDIOTAPING HOW-TO

- Both the Video and Audio Planning and Guidelines may be filled out, photocopied, and given to the respective individuals before your wedding day.

Video

- View the product before buying it. Check a sample tape for quality of coverage, movement, color, clarity, and sound.

- The least expensive type of videotaping uses only one camera in a more or less stationary position. The shots are taken as the action unfolds, in a straightforward manner. There's no postproduction work on the tape—no editing, sound dubbing, or special effects.

- Find out about any restrictions concerning videotaping at the ceremony site.

- Ask the videographer to attend the rehearsal to determine exactly where to position the camera(s) for the best possible results while taking into consideration the location of the bridal couple, their attendants, and the officiant during the ceremony, as well as the location of flowers, greenery, candelabra, etc.

- The rehearsal time also gives the videographer an understanding of your particular wedding ceremony so he can plan ahead for any special shots.

- Suggest to camera operators that they be as unobtrusive as possible during the ceremony.

Audio

- If the ceremony site is not equipped with an audiotaping system, use a hidden cassette recorder to record the service. Adequate results can be obtained with a quality recorder.

VIDEO ESTIMATE

OPTION #1   OPTION #2

Name _____   Name _____
Address _____   Address _____
Contact person _____   Contact person _____
Phone _____   Phone _____
Appointment date and time: Appointment date and time:

_____   _____

DESCRIPTION OF SERVICES   COST   DESCRIPTION OF SERVICES   COST

Number of hours _____   Number of hours _____
(tape length _____) $_____ (tape length _____) $_____
Number of cameras _____   Number of cameras _____
Planning: ❏ as it unfolds _____ Planning: ❏ as it unfolds _____
          ❏ tell a story   _____   ❏ tell a story   _____
Editing   _____ Editing   _____
Sound   _____ Sound   _____
   ❏ audio capability ❏ dubbing   ❏ audio capability ❏ dubbing
Special effects _____   _____ Special effects _____   _____
Extra cassettes: #_____ _____ Extra cassettes: #_____ _____
Other   Other

            NOTES   NOTES

Video choice: #_____ Date confirmed _____
Total cost _____ Deposit paid _____ Balance due _____ by _____
Date video will be ready _____

VIDEO PLANNING AND GUIDELINES

Wedding of _____ Phone _____

Ceremony site _____

Address _____

Contact person _____ Phone _____

Date _____ Time _____

Reception site _____

Address _____

Contact person _____ Phone _____

Date _____ Time _____

What to wear _____

Ceremony site restrictions _____
_____

Planning/staging

NOTES

AUDIO ESTIMATE

OPTION #1

Name _____

Address _____

Contact person _____

Phone _____

Appointment date and time:

_____

Taping is for: ❏ Ceremony only

              ❏ Reception only

              ❏ Both

Description of services   Cost

Number of hours _____ $_____

Number of copies _____ _____

Equipment rental _____ _____

   Taping   _____

   Sound   _____

Operator fee   _____

Other _____ _____

NOTES

OPTION #2

Name _____

Address _____

Contact person _____

Phone _____

Appointment date and time:

_____

Taping is for: ❏ Ceremony only

              ❏ Reception only

              ❏ Both

Description of services   Cost

Number of hours _____ $_____

Number of copies _____ _____

Equipment rental _____ _____

   Taping   _____

   Sound   _____

Operator fee   _____

Other _____ _____

NOTES

Audio choice: #_____ Date confirmed _____

Total cost _____ Deposit paid _____ Balance due _____ by _____

Date tapes will be ready _____

AUDIO PLANNING AND GUIDELINES

Wedding of _____ Phone _____

Ceremony site _____

Address _____

Contact person _____ Phone _____

Date _____ Time _____

Reception site _____

Address _____

Contact person _____ Phone _____

Date _____ Time _____

What to wear _____

Ceremony site restrictions _____

_____

_____

Planning:

NOTES

Housing and Transportation How-To

Out-of-Town Guests

- Accommodations for out-of-town guests can be arranged at a friend's home or at a hotel.

- Hotel and travel expenses for out-of-town guests are not the bride's or groom's responsibility.

- It is nice to provide entertainment for your out-of-town guests. This is a time to ask your friends for help. They could host a party before the wedding, an informal supper, a poolside party, a postreception party, or a tour of the area.

- Send the following to out-of-town guests one to two weeks before their planned arrival:

    —a copy of the Information List: Guest Housing and Transportation on page 176, listing where everyone is staying

    —a list of sight-seeing activities and maps of the area

    —agendas of all activities and maps to reach their locations

    —a list of needed clothes and leisure equipment

- If out-of-town guests are not driving their own cars, and if they have not reserved rental cars for their use on arrival, then you could arrange their transportation or make them aware of what is available.

Wedding Party Transportation

- Many different modes of transportation can be used for the bride, groom, parents, and attendants, from antique cars or horse-drawn carriages to limousines, privately owned cars, or whatever your imagination comes up with—antique trolley cars, bicycles, helicopters, or hot-air balloons.

- If possible, four or more vehicles should be reserved to provide transportation to the ceremony for the following: (a) the groom and best man, (b) the bridesmaids, (c) the bride's mother and honor attendant, and (d) the bride and her father.

- Transportation to the reception requires vehicles for the following: (a) the bride and groom, (b) the best man and honor attendant, (c) the bridesmaids and ushers, (d) the ring bearer and flower girl and their parents, and (e) the parents of both the bride and groom.

- To allow for any unforeseen scheduling changes, enlist the transportation service for a longer period of time than deemed necessary, as transportation services are tightly booked.

GUEST HOUSING AND TRANSPORTATION

Name of hotel/host _____

Address _____

    Rates _____ Phone _____

Guest(s) _____

Arrival date and time _____ Airline flight # _____

Departure date and time _____ Airline flight # _____

Driver to and from airport _____

Driver to and from wedding/reception _____

Name of hotel/host _____

Address _____

    Rates _____ Phone _____

Guest(s) _____

Arrival date and time _____ Airline flight # _____

Departure date and time _____ Airline flight # _____

Driver to and from airport _____

Driver to and from wedding/reception _____

Name of hotel/host _____

Address _____

    Rates _____ Phone _____

Guest(s) _____

Arrival date and time _____ Airline flight # _____

Departure date and time _____ Airline flight # _____

Driver to and from airport _____

Driver to and from wedding/reception _____

Name of hotel/host _____

Address _____

    Rates _____ Phone _____

Guest(s) _____

Arrival date and time _____ Airline flight # _____

Departure date and time _____ Airline flight # _____

Driver to and from airport _____

Driver to and from wedding/reception _____

Name of hotel/host _____

Address _____

    Rates _____ Phone _____

Guest(s) _____

Arrival date and time _____ Airline flight # _____

Departure date and time _____ Airline flight # _____

Driver to and from airport _____

Driver to and from wedding/reception _____

Information List: Guest Housing and Transportation

Guest(s) _____ Staying at room# _____
Driver to and from airport _____
Driver to and from wedding/reception _____

Guest(s) _____ Staying at room# _____
Driver to and from airport _____
Driver to and from wedding/reception _____

Guest(s) _____ Staying at room# _____
Driver to and from airport _____
Driver to and from wedding/reception _____

Guest(s) _____ Staying at room# _____
Driver to and from airport _____
Driver to and from wedding/reception _____

Guest(s) _____ Staying at room# _____
Driver to and from airport _____
Driver to and from wedding/reception _____

Guest(s) _____ Staying at room# _____
Driver to and from airport _____
Driver to and from wedding/reception _____

Guest(s) _____ Staying at room# _____
Driver to and from airport _____
Driver to and from wedding/reception _____

Guest(s) _____ Staying at room# _____
Driver to and from airport _____
Driver to and from wedding/reception _____

Guest(s) _____ Staying at room# _____
Driver to and from airport _____
Driver to and from wedding/reception _____

Transportation
Guidelines for Drivers

Guest(s) _____

Arrival date and time _____ Airline flight # _____

Staying at _____ Room # _____

Departure date and time _____ Airline flight # _____

Driver _____

Guest(s) _____

Arrival date and time _____ Airline flight # _____

Staying at _____ Room # _____

Departure date and time _____ Airline flight # _____

Driver _____

Guest(s) _____

Arrival date and time _____ Airline flight # _____

Staying at _____ Room # _____

Departure date and time _____ Airline flight # _____

Driver _____

Guest(s) _____

Arrival date and time _____ Airline flight # _____

Staying at _____ Room # _____

Departure date and time _____ Airline flight # _____

Driver _____

Guest(s) _____

Arrival date and time _____ Airline flight # _____

Staying at _____ Room # _____

Departure date and time _____ Airline flight # _____

Driver _____

Guest(s) _____

Arrival date and time _____ Airline flight # _____

Staying at _____ Room # _____

Departure date and time _____ Airline flight # _____

Driver _____

Guest(s) _____

Arrival date and time _____ Airline flight # _____

Staying at _____ Room # _____

Departure date and time _____ Airline flight # _____

Driver _____

Guest(s) _____

Arrival date and time _____ Airline flight # _____

Staying at _____ Room # _____

Departure date and time _____ Airline flight # _____

Driver _____

WEDDING PARTY TRANSPORTATION ESTIMATE

OPTION #1   OPTION #2

Option #1	Option #2
Name _____	Name _____
Address _____	Address _____
Contact person _____	Contact person _____
Phone _____	Phone _____
Type of vehicle _____	Type of vehicle _____
Number needed _____	Number needed _____
Length of service _____	Length of service _____
Per-mile cost _____	Per-mile cost _____
Hourly rate _____	Hourly rate _____
Overtime _____	Overtime _____
Wedding packages _____	Wedding packages _____

Choice #_____   Date confirmed _____

Total cost _____   Deposit paid _____   Balance due _____   by _____

WEDDING PARTY TRANSPORTATION GUIDELINES

Wedding of _____ Phone _____

Address _____

Wedding date _____

Ceremony site _____

Address _____

Contact person _____ Phone _____

Date _____ Time _____

Reception site _____

Address _____

Contact person _____ Phone _____

Date _____ Time _____

Type of vehicles _____ Number needed _____

Pickup Times

BEFORE WEDDING

Groom and parents _____ Time _____

Address _____ Phone _____

Groom's attendants _____ Time _____

Address _____ Phone _____

Bride and parents _____ Time _____

Address _____ Phone _____

Bride's attendants _____ Time _____

Address _____ Phone _____

Other _____ Time _____

Address _____ Phone _____

AFTER WEDDING

Destination _____ Time _____

Address _____ Phone _____

AFTER RECEPTION

Destination _____ Time _____

Address _____ Phone _____

RENTAL EQUIPMENT
HOW-TO

- The charge is usually based on a daily rate or a single-use price per item.

- A required security deposit generally serves to guarantee item availability.

- The deposit is refunded if items are returned in a satisfactory condition. A replacement cost is usually charged for any losses.

- Payment is generally required upon delivery or when you pick up any rented items.

- Delivery, setup, and pickup fees may also be charged.

EQUIPMENT LIST

Name _____

Address _____

Contact person _____ Phone _____

Qᴛʏ.   Cᴏsᴛ

Ceremony Accessories:

_____ _____ Wedding arch

_____ _____ Wedding canopy
(chuppah)

_____ _____ Latticework backdrops

_____ _____ Floor candelabra

_____ _____   3-light trinity

_____ _____   7-light, adjustable

_____ _____   9-light

_____ _____   15-light, spiral

_____ _____   15-light, fan

_____ _____   17-light, heart
shape

Aisle candelabra

_____ _____   clamp type

_____ _____   free-standing

_____ _____ Candles

_____ _____ Candlelighters

_____ _____ Kneeling bench

_____ _____ Floral baskets

Flower stands

_____ _____   8-inch

_____ _____   12-inch

_____ _____   16-inch

_____ _____   20-inch

_____ _____   24-inch

Aisle stanchions—posts
and chains

_____ _____ Aisle runners
(differing lengths)

_____ _____ Guest book stand

Chairs:

To determine the seating capacity of an area using theater style seating, divide the square footage of the area by 10.

_____ _____ Folding contour seat
and back

_____ _____ White wood with
padded seat

Tables:

When using the oblong banquet tables, divide the square feet of the area by 8. When using the round banquet tables, divide the square feet of the area by 10.

Oblong tables
(30" wide 29" high)

_____ _____   6' table seats 6–8

_____ _____   8' table seats 8–10

Round tables

_____ _____   24" table seats 2

_____ _____   36" table seats 4

_____ _____   48" table seats 6

_____ _____   60" table seats 8

_____ _____   72" table seats 10–
12

_____ _____ Heart-shaped tables—
excellent for cakes

_____ _____ Card tables (34"
square, 28" high)

Linens:

Long cloths

_____ _____ 54"x54" and 60"x 60" fit card table

_____ _____ 60"x120" fits 6' and 8' tables

Round cloths

_____ _____ 60" fits 24" to 36" round table

_____ _____ 72" drapes 24" round table to the floor; also fits 36" to 48" round table

_____ _____ 90" drapes 36" round table to the floor; also fits 48" to 60" round table

_____ _____ 100" drapes 48" round table to the floor; also fits 60" to 72" round table

_____ _____ 120" drapes 60" round table to the floor; also fits 72" round table

Specialty cloths (lace overlays)

_____ _____ 60"x60"

_____ _____ 60"x120"

_____ _____ 60" round

_____ _____ 72" round

_____ _____ 90" round

Napkins

_____ _____ cocktail

_____ _____ dinner

Table skirting (lace and solid):

Rental agencies either charge a flat fee per table or charge by the inch. Lace patterns are usually a bit more expensive. You'll need to know if you want three or all four sides covered. To determine the length of skirting needed for 4 sides: measure the perimeter of the table. For 3 sides: multiply the width by 2 and add the length of the table. For a round table: multiply 3.14 by the diameter of the table. Rental agencies will send enough skirting for the area to be covered, but it may be in more than one section. Just overlap the ends and continue pinning. Pins are usually included, but it's wise to also have a generous supply of T-pins (wig pins) to firmly secure the skirting to the table.

Skirting length

_____ _____ 6' table, 4 sides: 204" plus overlap

_____ _____ 6' table, 3 sides: 132" plus overlap

_____ _____ 8' table, 4 sides: 252" plus overlap

_____ _____ 60" round: 189" plus overlap

_____ _____ 72" round: 227" plus overlap

_____ _____ 90" round: 283" plus overlap

—— —— 100" round: 314" plus overlap

—— —— 120" round: 377" plus overlap

Flatware:

❑ Silverplate ❑ Stainless

—— —— Dinner knives
—— —— Dinner forks
—— —— Salad and dessert forks
—— —— Teaspoons
—— —— Soup spoons
—— —— Butter knives
—— —— Shrimp forks
—— —— Steak knives
—— —— Meat forks
—— —— Salad spoon and fork sets
—— —— Salad tongs
—— —— Serving spoons
—— —— Cake knife
—— —— Cake server

Dinnerware:

❑ China ❑ Glass ❑ Plastic

—— —— Dinner plates
—— —— Bread and butter plates
—— —— Salad plates
—— —— Cups
—— —— Saucers
—— —— Cereal/soup bowls
—— —— Fruit bowls
—— —— Creamer and sugar
—— —— Salt and pepper shakers

—— —— Vegetable bowls
—— —— Gravy boats
—— —— Platters

Glassware:

❑ Glass ❑ Plastic

Stemware

—— —— 4 1/2 oz. champagne
—— —— 6 1/2 oz. wine
—— —— 12 oz. goblet
—— —— parfait glass
—— —— sherbet glass

Glasses

—— —— 5 oz. juice glass
—— —— water glass
—— —— 4 oz. punch cup
—— —— Pitchers

Punch Fountains:

—— —— 3 gallon
—— —— 7 gallon

Punch Bowls:

(usually 3-gallon capacity)

❑ Silver ❑ Glass ❑ Plastic

—— —— with tray
—— —— without tray
—— —— Silver ladle
—— —— Plastic ladle

Coffee Makers and Servers:

Automatic coffee makers

—— —— 35-cup
—— —— 55-cup
—— —— 100-cup

Silver urns

_____ _____ 25-cup

_____ _____ 50-cup

_____ _____ tray

_____ _____ sugar and creamer

_____ _____ Silver coffee and tea
service: set of two
pots, tray, sugar
and creamer

_____ _____ Insulated coffee
pitchers

Miscellaneous Serving Pieces:

_____ _____ Silver bonbon dishes

_____ _____ Silver Revere bowls—
various sizes

_____ _____ Silver bread dishes

_____ _____ Silver relish dishes

_____ _____ Silver sugar tongs

_____ _____ Chafing dishes
❏ Silver ❏ Stainless

_____ _____ 2-quart

_____ _____ 4-quart

_____ _____ 8-quart

Food pans

full pan

_____ _____ 4-quart

_____ _____ 8-quart

half pan

_____ _____ 4-quart

_____ _____ 8-quart

1/3 pan

_____ _____ 4-quart

_____ _____ 8-quart

Bowls
❏ Stainless ❏ Plastic

_____ _____ 12-inch

_____ _____ 14-inch

_____ _____ 16-inch

_____ _____ 18-inch

_____ _____ 20-inch

_____ _____ 24-inch

_____ _____ Electric roasters

Electric hot plates

_____ _____ single burner

_____ _____ double burner

Barbecue

_____ _____ grills

_____ _____ equipment

_____ _____ Portable bar

_____ _____ Bar stools

_____ _____ Ice buckets

_____ _____ Ice tongs

_____ _____ Insulated coolers

_____ _____ Ice chests

Trays:

❏ Silver ❏ Chrome
❏ Stainless ❏ Plastic

_____ _____ 10" round

_____ _____ 12" round

_____ _____ 14" round

_____ _____ 16" round

_____ _____ 18" round

_____ _____ 20" round

_____ _____ 22" round

_____ _____ 13"x21" oval

_____ _____	15"x24" oval
_____ _____	10"x17" oblong
_____ _____	13"x19" oblong
_____ _____	14"x22" oblong
_____ _____	17"x23" oblong
_____ _____	Waiters' trays

Garden and Patio:

_____ _____ Floors: usually 4'x4' wood sections designed to be set up in any size area, indoors or outdoors on level surfaces. Divide the square footage of the area to be covered by the square footage of one section of wood to determine the number of sections you will need.

_____ _____ Stages, platform risers: usually in 3'X6' sections, excellent for head table, bandstands, and walkways.

Lighting and electrical

_____ _____ spotlights

_____ _____ pole lights

_____ _____ twinkle lights

_____ _____ tiki torches

_____ _____ floating candles

_____ _____ hurricane lights

_____ _____ extension cords

Heating

_____ _____ indoor electric heaters

_____ _____ outdoor propane heaters

Cooling

_____ _____ table fans

_____ _____ floor fans

_____ _____ portable air conditioners

Canopies

_____ _____ canopies: usually available in a variety of colors and sizes

_____ _____ side walls for canopies: usually rented by lineal foot, in solid or clear vinyl.

Umbrellas

_____ _____ with stand only

_____ _____ with stand and 48" round table

_____ _____ with stand and 60" round table

_____ _____ with stand and 72" round table

_____ _____ special linen (necessary for use on umbrella tables)

Guest Items:

_____ _____ Rollaway beds ❑ 30" ❑ 39" ❑ 48"

_____ _____	Baby crib	_____ _____ Mirror disc ball
_____ _____	Infant car seat	_____ _____ Movie projector
_____ _____	High chair	_____ _____ Slide projector
_____ _____	Stroller	_____ _____ Projector screen
_____ _____	Play pen	

Miscellaneous:

_____ _____ Garment rack

_____ _____ Garbage cans

_____ _____ Electric bug zapper

Total rental cost _____

Deposit _____

Balance due _____

Date due _____

EQUIPMENT DELIVERY AND PICKUP

Ceremony Site

BEFORE:

Contact person _____ Phone _____

Date _____ Time _____

Pickup _____

Delivery _____

Setup _____

Payment _____ When _____

AFTER:

Date _____ Time _____

Tear down _____

Return _____

Pickup _____

Reception Site

BEFORE:

Contact person _____ Phone _____

Date _____ Time _____

Pickup _____

Delivery _____

Setup _____

Payment _____ When _____

AFTER:

Date _____ Time _____

Tear down _____

Return _____

Pickup _____

HONEYMOON HOW-TO

- If your wedding is scheduled for late afternoon or evening, the groom will need to arrange for a nearby hotel for your wedding night.

- If you will be traveling out of town, consult with a travel agent, who can offer valuable tips on vacation sites, their available activities and weather probabilities, and take advantage of the best rates for hotel and travel accommodations.

- If you are flying, take a carry-on bag that contains all the essentials for a day.

- If you are driving a long distance, lock all luggage in the trunk as a deterrent to robbery.

- Carry a copy of your marriage certificate with you when traveling abroad, particularly if your passport is in your former name.

- Remember, do not overschedule. Your honeymoon is a time to get to know each other better.

- It's a nice gesture for you and your groom to telephone both your parents when you arrive at your travel destination. It will let them know you have arrived safely and will also offer another opportunity to thank them for the wedding.

HONEYMOON TRAVEL AND ACCOMMODATIONS

Travel agency _____

Address _____

Agent _____ Phone _____

Total cost _____ Amount due _____

Honeymoon dates: from _____ to _____

WEDDING NIGHT

Hotel _____

Address _____

Contact person_____ Phone _____

Room accommodations _____

Room #_____ Rate _____ Amount due_____ Reservations: ❑ Made
                                                            ❑ Confirmed

Date: Arrival_____ Departure _____

(Notes on wedding night accommodations: Arrange for snacks in your room. Ask to see the room ahead of time. Is it romantic? private?)

TRAVEL RESERVATIONS: AIRLINE, SHIP, RENTAL CAR

DATE	RATE	CARRIER/NUMBER	DEPARTURE/ARRIVAL	PHONE

Travel plans _____
Reservations: ❑ Made ❑ Confirmed Total cost _____ Amount due _____
Travel plans _____
Reservations: ❑ Made ❑ Confirmed Total cost _____ Amount due _____
Travel plans _____
Reservations: ❑ Made ❑ Confirmed Total cost _____ Amount due _____
Travel plans _____
Reservations: ❑ Made ❑ Confirmed Total cost _____ Amount due _____

HOTEL RESERVATIONS

Hotel _____

Address _____

Contact person _____ Phone _____

Room accommodations _____

Transportation _____

Room #_____ Rate _____ Amount due _____ Reservations: ❑ Made ❑ Confirmed

Date: Arrival _____ Departure _____

Hotel _____

Address _____

Contact person _____ Phone _____

Room accommodations _____

Transportation _____

Room #_____ Rate _____ Amount due _____ Reservations: ❑ Made ❑ Confirmed

Date: Arrival _____ Departure _____

Hotel _____

Address _____

Contact person _____ Phone _____

Room accommodations _____

Transportation _____

Room #_____ Rate _____ Amount due _____ Reservations: ❑ Made ❑ Confirmed

Date: Arrival _____ Departure _____

Hotel _____

Address _____

Contact person _____ Phone _____

Room accommodations _____

Transportation _____

Room #_____ Rate _____ Amount due _____ Reservations: ❑ Made ❑ Confirmed

Date: Arrival _____ Departure _____

For Travel Abroad

Necessary papers:

❑ Passports ❑ Visa ❑ Marriage License ❑ Travelers Checks

Inoculations needed:

_____ _____

_____ _____

_____ _____

Special Parties

SPECIAL PARTIES HOW-TO

- You'll be of great help to the hosts and hostesses who are planning the various special parties if you fill out and photocopy for them the appropriate guest lists in this section. Guest lists are provided here for three bridal showers, the bridal luncheon, the preceremony buffet, the bachelor party, and the rehearsal dinner.

- You can also provide the hosts and hostesses with copies of the estimate and planning worksheets included here.

Bridal Showers

- Traditionally, bridal showers are given by friends rather than relatives, although relatives can help.

- Today, showers often are given not only for the bride but also for the bride and groom together.

- Since you may be given more than one bridal shower, you might suggest a different guest list for each party.

- When some guests, including family members and bridal attendants, are invited to attend more than one shower, you may suggest they bring a gift to only one.

- Guests may contact the various hostesses for gift suggestions.

- At the showers, have someone record the gifts and who gave them, thus helping you avoid mistakes when you send thank-you notes.

- Make "bouquets" from the ribbons and bows for you and your bridal attendants to practice with at the wedding rehearsal.

Bridal Luncheon

- The bride may host a luncheon for her attendants, her mother, and the groom's mother. The maid/matron of honor, a family member, or a close friend could host this luncheon as well. It should be held a week or two before the wedding.

- If time commitments prohibit a luncheon, it's appropriate to schedule it in the evening, perhaps the same time as the bachelor party.

- You can hold the luncheon at home, in a restaurant, or at a club, or even have a picnic in the park—wherever your imagination leads.

- The degree of formality is strictly your choice.

Bachelor Party

- The groom, the best man, a family member, or a close friend may host the bachelor party for the groom and his attendants.

- The party theme can be creative—golf, sailing, fishing, hunting, backpacking, etc.

Rehearsal Dinner

- The rehearsal dinner provides a special time for the bride and groom to express their appreciation to everyone.

- Traditionally the groom's parents host the rehearsal dinner. The bride's family, a close relative, or a special friend may host the dinner if the groom's parents are unable to do so.

- It is usually a sit-down dinner held immediately following the rehearsal. It may be held at home or in a restaurant, resort, or club.

- If the hosts are from out of town, you may facilitate their search for a dinner site by offering suggestions on available places to hold the dinner. Also, send copies of the menus from each place.

- The style of your wedding often sets the tone for the dinner—from a formal dinner with place cards and centerpieces to a simple, casual get-together.

- If it's being held the night before the wedding, schedule the dinner for an early hour to allow everyone a good night's sleep.

- The following should be invited to the dinner: the bride and groom and their parents; all members of the bridal party and their spouses or fiancés;

the parents of any children in the wedding party; and the officiant and his or her spouse or fiancé.

- Others to consider inviting are the organist and soloist(s) and their spouses or fiancés, the wedding coordinator and spouse or fiancé, out-of-town guests, and special friends.

Preceremony Buffet

- A preceremony buffet gives everyone an opportunity to relax while also providing a nourishing boost for the remainder of the day. Too often everyone ends up eating take-out food from a fast-food restaurant because of a lack of time and planning.

- A friend might plan, prepare, and serve this special buffet for you.

- You might schedule the buffet at the bride's home or at the ceremony site, whichever is more convenient.

- The buffet could be served during the last thirty to forty-five minutes prior to the ceremony, especially when you have arrived early for picture-taking.

BRIDAL SHOWER GUEST LIST

Hostess _____ Phone _____

Address _____

Date _____ Time _____ Number of guests_____

Yes/No (RSVP)	Name and Address	Phone
☐ ☐	_____	
☐ ☐	_____	
☐ ☐	_____	
☐ ☐	_____	
☐ ☐	_____	
☐ ☐	_____	
☐ ☐	_____	
☐ ☐	_____	
☐ ☐	_____	
☐ ☐	_____	
☐ ☐	_____	
☐ ☐	_____	
☐ ☐	_____	
☐ ☐	_____	
☐ ☐	_____	
☐ ☐	_____	
☐ ☐	_____	
☐ ☐	_____	
☐ ☐	_____	
☐ ☐	_____	
☐ ☐	_____	
☐ ☐	_____	
☐ ☐	_____	
☐ ☐	_____	
☐ ☐	_____	
☐ ☐	_____	

BRIDAL SHOWER GUEST LIST

Hostess _____ Phone _____

Address _____

Date _____ Time _____ Number of guests_____

Yes / No (RSVP)   NAME AND ADDRESS   PHONE

❑ ❑ _____

❑ ❑ _____

❑ ❑ _____

❑ ❑ _____

❑ ❑ _____

❑ ❑ _____

❑ ❑ _____

❑ ❑ _____

❑ ❑ _____

❑ ❑ _____

❑ ❑ _____

❑ ❑ _____

❑ ❑ _____

❑ ❑ _____

❑ ❑ _____

❑ ❑ _____

❑ ❑ _____

❑ ❑ _____

❑ ❑ _____

❑ ❑ _____

❑ ❑ _____

❑ ❑ _____

❑ ❑ _____

❑ ❑ _____

❑ ❑ _____

BRIDAL SHOWER GUEST LIST

Hostess _____ Phone _____

Address _____

Date _____ Time _____ Number of guests_____

YES / NO (RSVP)	NAME AND ADDRESS	PHONE
☐ ☐	_____	
☐ ☐	_____	
☐ ☐	_____	
☐ ☐	_____	
☐ ☐	_____	
☐ ☐	_____	
☐ ☐	_____	
☐ ☐	_____	
☐ ☐	_____	
☐ ☐	_____	
☐ ☐	_____	
☐ ☐	_____	
☐ ☐	_____	
☐ ☐	_____	
☐ ☐	_____	
☐ ☐	_____	
☐ ☐	_____	
☐ ☐	_____	
☐ ☐	_____	
☐ ☐	_____	
☐ ☐	_____	
☐ ☐	_____	
☐ ☐	_____	
☐ ☐	_____	

BRIDAL LUNCHEON GUEST LIST

Hostess _____ Phone _____

Address _____

Date _____ Time _____ Number of guests_____

Yes/No (RSVP)	Name and Address	Phone
☐ ☐	_____	
☐ ☐	_____	
☐ ☐	_____	
☐ ☐	_____	
☐ ☐	_____	
☐ ☐	_____	
☐ ☐	_____	
☐ ☐	_____	
☐ ☐	_____	
☐ ☐	_____	
☐ ☐	_____	
☐ ☐	_____	
☐ ☐	_____	
☐ ☐	_____	
☐ ☐	_____	
☐ ☐	_____	
☐ ☐	_____	
☐ ☐	_____	
☐ ☐	_____	
☐ ☐	_____	
☐ ☐	_____	
☐ ☐	_____	
☐ ☐	_____	
☐ ☐	_____	

BRIDAL LUNCHEON ESTIMATE

OPTION #1

Name _____

Address _____

Contact person _____

Phone _____

Date _____ Time_____

Number of guests _____

DESCRIPTION OF MENU CHOICES   COST

_____

_____

_____

_____

DECORATIONS (COLOR OF TABLE LINENS,
CENTERPIECES, CANDLES, ETC.)

_____

_____

_____

SUGGESTED SEATING

_____

_____

_____

Cost of separate room_____

Estimated total cost _____

Gratuity included: ❑ Yes ❑ No

OPTION #2

Name _____

Address _____

Contact person _____

Phone _____

Date _____ Time_____

Number of guests _____

DESCRIPTION OF MENU CHOICES   COST

_____

_____

_____

_____

DECORATIONS (COLOR OF TABLE LINENS,
CENTERPIECES, CANDLES, ETC.)

_____

_____

_____

SUGGESTED SEATING

_____

_____

_____

Cost of separate room_____

Estimated total cost _____

Gratuity included: ❑ Yes ❑ No

Choice #_____ Date confirmed _____

Total cost _____ Deposit paid _____ Balance due _____ by_____

Scheduled date _____ Time _____

BRIDAL LUNCHEON MENU

APPETIZER

_____
_____
_____

SALAD/SOUP

_____
_____
_____

ENTRÉE

_____
_____
_____

DESSERT

_____
_____
_____

BEVERAGE

_____
_____
_____

NOTES

PRECEREMONY BUFFET
GUEST LIST

Buffet site _____ Room # _____

Hostess _____ Phone _____

Address _____

Date _____ Time _____ Number of guests_____

Yes / No (RSVP)	Name and Address	Phone
☐ ☐	_____	
☐ ☐	_____	
☐ ☐	_____	
☐ ☐	_____	
☐ ☐	_____	
☐ ☐	_____	
☐ ☐	_____	
☐ ☐	_____	
☐ ☐	_____	
☐ ☐	_____	
☐ ☐	_____	
☐ ☐	_____	
☐ ☐	_____	
☐ ☐	_____	
☐ ☐	_____	
☐ ☐	_____	
☐ ☐	_____	
☐ ☐	_____	
☐ ☐	_____	
☐ ☐	_____	
☐ ☐	_____	

PRECEREMONY BUFFET PLANNING

Buffet site _____ Room # _____

Hostess _____ Phone _____

Address _____

Date _____ Time _____ Number of guests _____

Menu Planning

_____

_____

_____

_____

_____

Dishes, Glassware, Flatware, Chairs, Tables, Linens, etc.

_____

_____

_____

_____

_____

Setup and Cleanup

_____

_____

_____

_____

_____

BACHELOR PARTY
GUEST LIST

Event site _____

Address _____

Contact person _____ Phone _____

Date _____ Time _____ Number of guests _____

YES / NO (RSVP)	NAME AND ADDRESS	PHONE
☐ ☐		
☐ ☐		
☐ ☐		
☐ ☐		
☐ ☐		
☐ ☐		
☐ ☐		
☐ ☐		
☐ ☐		
☐ ☐		
☐ ☐		
☐ ☐		
☐ ☐		
☐ ☐		
☐ ☐		
☐ ☐		
☐ ☐		
☐ ☐		
☐ ☐		
☐ ☐		
☐ ☐		

BACHELOR PARTY ESTIMATE

OPTION #1	OPTION #2

Name _____   Name _____

Address _____   Address _____

Contact person _____   Contact person _____

Phone _____   Phone _____

Date _____ Time _____   Date _____ Time _____

Number of guests _____   Number of guests _____

THEME

_____

NEEDED EQUIPMENT

Cost of separate room _____   Cost of separate room _____

Estimated total cost _____   Estimated total cost _____

Gratuity included: ❑ Yes ❑ No   Gratuity included: ❑ Yes ❑ No

Choice #_____ Date confirmed _____

Total cost _____ Deposit paid _____ Balance due _____ by_____

Scheduled date _____ Time _____

BACHELOR PARTY MENU

APPETIZER

_____
_____
_____

SALAD/SOUP

_____
_____
_____

ENTRÉE

_____
_____
_____

DESSERT

_____
_____
_____

BEVERAGE

_____
_____
_____

NOTES

REHEARSAL DINNER
GUEST LIST

Dinner site _____

Address _____

Contact person _____ Phone _____

Hosts _____ Phone _____

Date _____ Time _____ Number of guests_____

YES / NO (RSVP)   NAME AND ADDRESS   PHONE

☐ ☐ _____

☐ ☐ _____

☐ ☐ _____

☐ ☐ _____

☐ ☐ _____

☐ ☐ _____

☐ ☐ _____

☐ ☐ _____

☐ ☐ _____

☐ ☐ _____

☐ ☐ _____

☐ ☐ _____

☐ ☐ _____

☐ ☐ _____

☐ ☐ _____

☐ ☐ _____

☐ ☐ _____

☐ ☐ _____

☐ ☐ _____

☐ ☐ _____

REHEARSAL DINNER ESTIMATE

<table>
<tr><td align="center">OPTION #1</td><td align="center">OPTION #2</td></tr>
</table>

OPTION #1	OPTION #2
Name _____	Name _____
Address _____	Address _____
Contact person _____	Contact person _____
Phone _____	Phone _____
Date _____ Time_____	Date _____ Time_____
Number of guests _____	Number of guests _____

DESCRIPTION OF MENU CHOICES COST	DESCRIPTION OF MENU CHOICES COST
_____	_____
_____	_____
_____	_____
_____	_____

DECORATIONS (COLOR OF TABLE LINENS, CENTERPIECES, CANDLES, ETC.)	DECORATIONS (COLOR OF TABLE LINENS, CENTERPIECES, CANDLES, ETC.)
_____	_____
_____	_____
_____	_____
_____	_____

SUGGESTED SEATING	SUGGESTED SEATING
_____	_____
_____	_____
_____	_____
_____	_____

Cost of separate room _____	Cost of separate room _____
Estimated total cost _____	Estimated total cost _____
Gratuity included: ❏ Yes ❏ No	Gratuity included: ❏ Yes ❏ No

Choice #_____ Date confirmed _____

Total cost _____ Deposit paid _____ Balance due _____ by_____

Scheduled date _____ Time _____

REHEARSAL DINNER MENU

APPETIZER

_____

_____

_____

SALAD/SOUP

_____

_____

_____

ENTRÉE

_____

_____

_____

DESSERT

_____

_____

_____

BEVERAGE

_____

_____

_____

NOTES

REHEARSAL DINNER PROGRAM

BEFORE DINNER

_____

_____

_____

DURING DINNER

_____

_____

_____

AFTER DINNER

_____

_____

_____

SPECIAL PRESENTATIONS

_____

_____

_____

BRIDE AND GROOM'S APPRECIATION

_____

_____

_____

Personal

BRIDE'S MEDICAL HOW-TO

- Make an appointment with your doctor for a physical examination at least three months prior to your wedding.

- This would be a time to discuss the various forms of contraceptives with your physician. Your personal health, religious values, and length of intended use will all figure into the decision of which form of contraceptive to use.

- Your doctor may also be able to answer other questions you have about the marriage relationship.

BRIDE'S MEDICAL RECORD

MEDICAL DOCTORS

Specialty _____

Name _____

Address _____

Phone _____

Chart # _____

Specialty _____

Name _____

Address _____

Phone _____

Chart # _____

Specialty _____

Name _____

Address _____

Phone _____

Chart # _____

Specialty _____

Name _____

Address _____

Phone _____

Chart # _____

Specialty _____

Name _____

Address _____

Phone _____

Chart # _____

MEDICAL INSURANCE

Company _____

Policy #_____

DENTAL INSURANCE

Company _____

Policy #_____

PERSONAL HISTORY

Birth weight_____ length _____

Blood type _____ Rh _____

Present weight _____ height _____

Blood pressure _____ Heart rate _____

Eyes: left _____ right _____

Contacts _____ Glasses _____

Ears: left _____ right _____

HAVE YOU EVER HAD:

YES/NO

❑ ❑ allergies   ❑ ❑ hives

❑ ❑ anemia   ❑ ❑ kidney trouble

❑ ❑ arthritis   ❑ ❑ measles

❑ ❑ asthma   ❑ ❑ menstrual cramps

❑ ❑ chicken pox   ❑ ❑ migraine headaches

❑ ❑ concussion   ❑ ❑ mononucleosis

❑ ❑ diabetes   ❑ ❑ mumps

❑ ❑ eczema   ❑ ❑ pneumonia

❑ ❑ emotional problems ❑ ❑ polio

❑ ❑ epilepsy   ❑ ❑ rheumatic fever

❑ ❑ frequent fainting❑ ❑ severe sinus trouble

❑ ❑ heart murmur   ❑ ❑ chronic sore throats

❑ ❑ hepatitis   ❑ ❑ tuberculosis

❑ ❑ hernia   ❑ ❑ whooping cough

❑ ❑ other _____

IMMUNIZATIONS   DATE   BOOSTER

DTP (diphtheria, tetanus, pertussis)

_____ _____

TD (tetanus, diphtheria, adult type)

Measles   _____ _____

Rubella   _____ _____

Mumps   _____ _____

Polio   _____ _____

Smallpox   _____ _____

Other   _____ _____

SKIN TESTS
   histoplasmosis   _____   _____
   tuberculosis   _____   _____
   valley fever   _____   _____
   other
_____   _____   _____

MEDICATIONS YOU ARE NOW TAKING

NAME	DOSAGE	FREQUENCY
_____	_____	_____
_____	_____	_____
_____	_____	_____
_____	_____	_____

X RAYS

DATE	HOSPITAL	REASON
_____	_____	_____
_____	_____	_____
_____	_____	_____

ALLERGIES

ALLERGY		REACTION
_____		_____
_____		_____
_____		_____
_____		_____

HOSPITALIZATIONS

DATE	HOSPITAL	REASON
_____	_____	_____
_____	_____	_____
_____	_____	_____
_____	_____	_____

MENSTRUAL PERIOD
Age at first menses _____
Length of monthly cycle _____
Average length of period _____
Type of flow (heavy or light) _____
Other _____

PRESENT MEDICAL TREATMENT
_____
_____
_____
_____

OTHER INFORMATION
_____
_____
_____
_____

Family History

RELATIONSHIP TO YOU	SERIOUS ILLNESSES EXPERIENCED (HEART DISEASE, HYPERTENSION, DIABETES, CANCER, ETC.)	IF DECEASED AGE AT DEATH	CAUSE OF DEATH
Mother	_____	____	_____
Father	_____	____	_____
Maternal grandmother	_____	____	_____
Maternal grandfather	_____	____	_____
Paternal grandmother	_____	____	_____
Paternal grandfather	_____	____	_____
Brothers and sisters	_____	____	_____
_____	_____	____	_____
_____	_____	____	_____
_____	_____	____	_____
Others	_____	____	_____
_____	_____	____	_____
_____	_____	____	_____

GROOM'S MEDICAL RECORD

MEDICAL DOCTORS

Specialty _____
Name _____
Address _____
Phone _____
Chart # _____

Specialty _____
Name _____
Address _____
Phone _____
Chart # _____

Specialty _____
Name _____
Address _____
Phone _____
Chart # _____

Specialty _____
Name _____
Address _____
Phone _____
Chart # _____

Specialty _____
Name _____
Address _____
Phone _____
Chart # _____

MEDICAL INSURANCE

Company _____
Policy # _____

DENTAL INSURANCE

Company _____
Policy # _____

PERSONAL HISTORY

Birth weight _____ length _____
Blood type _____ Rh _____
Present weight _____ height _____
Blood pressure _____ Heart rate _____
Eyes: left _____ right _____
Contacts _____ Glasses _____
Ears: left _____ right _____

HAVE YOU EVER HAD:

Yes/No

☐ ☐ allergies   ☐ ☐ hives
☐ ☐ anemia   ☐ ☐ kidney trouble
☐ ☐ arthritis   ☐ ☐ measles
☐ ☐ asthma   ☐ ☐ menstrual cramps
☐ ☐ chicken pox   ☐ ☐ migraine headaches
☐ ☐ concussion   ☐ ☐ mononucleosis
☐ ☐ diabetes   ☐ ☐ mumps
☐ ☐ eczema   ☐ ☐ pneumonia
☐ ☐ emotional problems ☐ ☐ polio
☐ ☐ epilepsy   ☐ ☐ rheumatic fever
☐ ☐ frequent fainting ☐ ☐ severe sinus trouble
☐ ☐ heart murmur   ☐ ☐ chronic sore throats
☐ ☐ hepatitis   ☐ ☐ tuberculosis
☐ ☐ hernia   ☐ ☐ whooping cough
☐ ☐ other _____

IMMUNIZATIONS	DATE	BOOSTER
DTP (diphtheria, tetanus, pertussis)	_____	_____
TD (tetanus, diphtheria, adult type)		
Measles	_____	_____
Rubella	_____	_____
Mumps	_____	_____
Polio	_____	_____
Smallpox	_____	_____
Other	_____	_____

SKIN TESTS

   histoplasmosis   _____ _____

   tuberculosis   _____ _____

   valley fever   _____ _____

   other

_____ _____ _____

MEDICATIONS YOU ARE NOW TAKING

NAME	DOSAGE	FREQUENCY
_____	_____	_____
_____	_____	_____
_____	_____	_____

X RAYS

DATE	HOSPITAL	REASON
_____	_____	_____
_____	_____	_____
_____	_____	_____
_____	_____	_____

ALLERGIES

ALLERGY	REACTION
_____	_____
_____	_____
_____	_____
_____	_____

HOSPITALIZATIONS

DATE	HOSPITAL	REASON
_____	_____	_____
_____	_____	_____
_____	_____	_____
_____	_____	_____

OTHER INFORMATION

_____

_____

_____

_____

PRESENT MEDICAL TREATMENT

_____

_____

_____

_____

_____

_____

_____

_____

Family History

RELATIONSHIP TO YOU	SERIOUS ILLNESSES EXPERIENCED (HEART DISEASE, HYPERTENSION, DIABETES, CANCER, ETC.)	IF DECEASED AGE AT DEATH	CAUSE OF DEATH
Mother	_____	_____	_____
Father	_____	_____	_____
Maternal grandmother	_____	_____	_____
Maternal grandfather	_____	_____	_____
Paternal grandmother	_____	_____	_____
Paternal grandfather	_____	_____	_____
Brothers and sisters	_____	_____	_____
_____	_____	_____	_____
_____	_____	_____	_____
Others	_____	_____	_____
_____	_____	_____	_____
_____	_____	_____	_____

Marriage License How-To

- All states require a marriage license. Regulations for obtaining a license vary from state to state.

- If your state requires blood tests to be taken, have verification of the results in hand when applying for your license.

- Proof of age or parental consent is necessary when making application for your license. Your driver's license, birth certificate, baptismal record, or adoption records can be used to show your age.

- If you need to show proof of citizenship, you may use your naturalization certificate, immigration record, adoption records, or passport.

- Find out if your state has a waiting period before the license is valid and you can marry; also check other timing requirements included in the license.

MARRIAGE LICENSE REQUIREMENTS

County clerk's office _____

Address _____

Date _____ Time _____ Phone _____

Waiting period required _____

License is valid for _____ days.

Fee_____

Requirements

❑ Certificate of verification for blood tests

❑ Proof of age or parental consent

❑ Proof of citizenship

❑ Driver's license

❑ Other _____

NEWSPAPER ANNOUNCEMENT
HOW-TO

- Send your announcement to the groom's and your hometown newspapers.

- Some papers have a policy whereby only one announcement is printed—either the engagement or the wedding. Decide which announcement you prefer.

- Secure a submission form from the lifestyles (or society) editor of the paper. An announcement will be written from the information you submit on the form. If a form is not available, study the announcements that appear in the paper and style yours accordingly.

- Before submitting a photograph with your announcement, check with the newspaper on their size preference. Many request a glossy 8-by-10-inch black-and-white print.

- Engagements are usually announced by the parents of the bride, a close relative, guardian, or friend.

- Designate a release date for the announcement if your engagement is to be announced at a surprise party.

- When the bride has been married before, it is better for her to forgo an engagement announcement. She can, however, announce the wedding after it has occurred.

- Include your address and phone number in case the editor needs to verify any information you send.

- If the engagement is broken after it has been announced, you will need to send a notice to any newspaper that carried your formal announcement. Either of the following examples may be used to give notice to the paper:

    Mr. and Mrs. _____ announce that the marriage of their daughter, _____, to Mr. _____ will not take place.

    The engagement of Ms. _____ and Mr. _____ will not take place.

NEWSPAPER ANNOUNCEMENT

Newspaper _____

Address _____

Lifestyles editor _____ Phone _____

To announce: ❑ Wedding ❑ Engagement ❑ Both

Wedding date _____

INFORMATION	BRIDE	GROOM
Names in full	_____	_____
Parents' names	_____	_____
Parents' address	_____	_____
Schools attended	_____	_____
Special clubs	_____	_____
Honors	_____	_____
Military service	_____	_____
Employment	_____	_____
Ceremony site	_____	_____
Reception site	_____	_____

Names of bridal party members (and their relationship to the bride or groom)

_____

_____

Description of bridal gown _____

_____

Description of bridal attendants' dresses _____

_____

Names of: Officiant _____ Soloist(s) _____

Honeymoon trip _____

Residence after wedding (city and state) _____

Financial/Legal How-To

- Getting married means changes in your legal marital status on legal and financial documents, including changes in name, address, and beneficiaries.

- Although brides are not required legally to change their names to that of the husbands, this is a long established custom that is followed by most women being married.

- Today some women, because of already established careers or to better maintain their own personal identity, are choosing not to follow this custom. They are retaining their former names, or using their former names professionally and their husbands' names socially, or using a hyphenated combination of both of their names.

- Whatever name you choose, be consistent to avoid confusion.

FINANCIAL/LEGAL CHECKLIST

Under the appropriate heading, indicate the specific changes to be made.
M = marital status   N = name   A = address   B = beneficiary

	Bride				Groom			
	M	N	A	B	M	N	A	B
Driver's license	☐	☐	☐	☐	☐	☐	☐	☐
Social security	☐	☐	☐	☐	☐	☐	☐	☐
Professional records	☐	☐	☐	☐	☐	☐	☐	☐
Employee records	☐	☐	☐	☐	☐	☐	☐	☐
School records	☐	☐	☐	☐	☐	☐	☐	☐
Checking accounts	☐	☐	☐	☐	☐	☐	☐	☐
Savings accounts	☐	☐	☐	☐	☐	☐	☐	☐
IRAs	☐	☐	☐	☐	☐	☐	☐	☐
Safe-deposit box	☐	☐	☐	☐	☐	☐	☐	☐
Loans	☐	☐	☐	☐	☐	☐	☐	☐
Stocks and bonds	☐	☐	☐	☐	☐	☐	☐	☐
Wills	☐	☐	☐	☐	☐	☐	☐	☐
Leases	☐	☐	☐	☐	☐	☐	☐	☐
Property titles	☐	☐	☐	☐	☐	☐	☐	☐
Insurance	☐	☐	☐	☐	☐	☐	☐	☐
Taxes	☐	☐	☐	☐	☐	☐	☐	☐
Credit cards	☐	☐	☐	☐	☐	☐	☐	☐
Car registration	☐	☐	☐	☐	☐	☐	☐	☐
Voter registration	☐	☐	☐	☐	☐	☐	☐	☐
Passport	☐	☐	☐	☐	☐	☐	☐	☐
Mail delivery	☐	☐	☐	☐	☐	☐	☐	☐
Business cards	☐	☐	☐	☐	☐	☐	☐	☐
Magazines/periodicals	☐	☐	☐	☐	☐	☐	☐	☐
Business stationery	☐	☐	☐	☐	☐	☐	☐	☐

Your driver's license and/or marriage certificate may be needed to effect some of these changes.

SETTING UP HOUSE HOW-TO

Where to Live

- Questions to ask as you plan for setting up house include:

  —How much will you be able to afford in monthly payments?

  —Will a location you're considering be convenient to all your activities?

  —Will it provide a sense of comfort and security—a feeling of being "at home"?

Home Furnishings

- If you are buying major furnishings, buy the best you can afford.

- Consider multifunctional and modular pieces to avoid overcrowding your apartment or house.

- Shop for bargains as you accessorize your new home. You can create a pleasing atmosphere without spending a lot of money.

- When you buy, realize that you will probably live with whatever you purchase for a longer period of time than you may have planned—so be sure you like it.

- If you or your fiancé has existing household furnishings, use the Keep or Toss worksheet as you decide how to blend your possessions.

Moving

- Your new address and apartment number are needed for acquiring utility services.

- Check with each utility several days before moving in, and pay required fees.

- You can either move yourself or hire professionals. It's better to hire professional movers if you are moving a great distance or have many possessions.

RENTAL HOUSING CHECKLIST

Name _____

Address _____

Contact person _____ Phone _____

Apartment # _____ Date available _____

Questions to Ask

1. Is the location convenient to work? ❑ Yes ❑ No   to school? ❑ Yes ❑ No
   to church? ❑ Yes ❑ No   to shopping? ❑ Yes ❑ No
   to entertainment? ❑ Yes ❑ No

2. Is there a lease? ❑ Yes ❑ No   If so, for how long?_____
   Can it be broken? ❑ Yes ❑ No Sublet? ❑ Yes ❑ No

3. What are the move-in costs? First month _____ Last month _____
   Security deposit _____ Cleaning deposit _____ Pet deposit _____

4. How often is the rent raised? _____

5. Can the rent be raised unexpectedly? ❑ Yes ❑ No

6. Are there laundry facilities? ❑ Yes ❑ No   Storage facilities? ❑ Yes ❑ No

7. Is someone readily available for maintenance needs?
   ❑ Yes (Name _____ Phone _____) ❑ No

8. Are there any security provisions? ❑ Yes ❑ No

9. What is included in the monthly rent? Water ❑ Yes ❑ No Gas ❑ Yes ❑ No
   Electricity ❑ Yes ❑ No Parking ❑ Yes (# of spaces _____) ❑ No
   Trash collection ❑ Yes ❑ No

10. If utility payments are not included in the monthly rent, what are the average
    monthly utility bills?
    Water _____ Gas _____ Electricity _____

What are the heaviest monthly usage payments?
Water_____ Gas_____ Electricity_____

11. Are you allowed to make any improvements such as hang pictures? ❑ Yes ❑ No
Install shelves? ❑ Yes ❑ No Other _____? ❑ Yes ❑ No

12. Are the appliances in good working order? ❑ Yes ❑ No

13. Are there any leaks in the plumbing? ❑ Yes ❑ No

14. Is the construction sound? ❑ Yes ❑ No

15. Can the neighbors be heard through the walls or ceiling/floor? ❑ Yes ❑ No

16. Is it free of household pests? ❑ Yes ❑ No

17. Are there any restrictions against children? ❑ Yes ❑ No

18. Are there any restrictions against pets? ❑ Yes ❑ No

19. What recreational facilities are offered?

Rented: ❑ Yes (Move-in date_____) ❑ No
Utility Setup

Water: turn-on date _____ fee _____

Gas: turn-on date _____ fee _____

Electricity: turn-on date _____ fee _____

Trash collection: turn-on date _____ fee _____

Phone service: turn-on date _____ fee _____

_____: turn-on date _____ fee _____

MOVING ESTIMATE

Your new address _____ Apartment #_____

City _____ State _____ Zip _____

Your new phone _____

Truck or Trailer Rental

ESTIMATE #1

Name _____

Address _____

Contact person _____ Phone _____

Cost: Per hour _____ Per day _____ Deposit _____

    Payment ❏ Cash ❏ Credit card Balance due _____

Pickup: Date _____ Time _____ Place _____

Return: Date _____ Time _____ Place _____

Confirmed: ❏ Yes ❏ No

ESTIMATE #2

Name _____

Address _____

Contact person _____ Phone _____

Cost: Per hour _____ Per day _____ Deposit _____

    Payment ❏ Cash ❏ Credit card Balance due _____

Pickup: Date _____ Time _____ Place _____

Return: Date _____ Time _____ Place _____

Confirmed: ❏ Yes ❏ No

ESTIMATE #3

Name _____

Address _____

Contact person _____ Phone _____

Cost: Per hour _____ Per day _____ Deposit _____

    Payment ❏ Cash ❏ Credit card Balance due _____

Pickup: Date _____ Time _____ Place _____

Return: Date _____ Time _____ Place _____

Confirmed: ❏ Yes ❏ No

Professional Movers

Name _____

Address _____

Contact person _____ Phone _____

Cost, per estimated weight _____ Deposit _____

    Payment ❑ Cash ❑ Credit card   Balance due _____

Insurance coverage _____

Dates: Packing _____ Loading _____ Delivery _____

Confirmed: ❑ Yes ❑ No

Driver of truck _____ Phone _____

ESTIMATE #2

Name _____

Address _____

Contact person _____ Phone _____

Cost, per estimated weight _____ Deposit _____

    Payment ❑ Cash ❑ Credit card   Balance due _____

Insurance coverage _____

Dates: Packing _____ Loading _____ Delivery _____

Confirmed: ❑ Yes ❑ No

Driver of truck _____ Phone _____

ESTIMATE #3

Name _____

Address _____

Contact person _____ Phone _____

Cost, per estimated weight _____ Deposit _____

    Payment ❑ Cash ❑ Credit card   Balance due _____

Insurance coverage _____

Dates: Packing _____ Loading _____ Delivery _____

Confirmed: ❑ Yes ❑ No

Driver of truck _____ Phone _____

NOTES

HOME FURNISHINGS
PURCHASE PLAN

Style _____

Colors _____

ROOM	ITEM	COST
Living	_____	_____
	_____	_____
	_____	_____
	_____	_____
	_____	_____
	_____	_____
	_____	_____
	_____	_____
	_____	_____
	_____	_____
	_____	_____
	_____	_____
	_____	_____
	_____	_____
	_____	_____
	_____	_____
Dining	_____	_____
	_____	_____
	_____	_____
	_____	_____
	_____	_____
	_____	_____
	_____	_____
Bedroom	_____	_____
	_____	_____
	_____	_____
	_____	_____
	_____	_____
	_____	_____
	_____	_____

Bedroom/study

Kitchen

Bathroom

Bathroom

Other

KEEP OR TOSS

Room	Item	Bride's	Groom's	Keep	Toss
Living	_____	☐	☐	☐	☐
	_____	☐	☐	☐	☐
	_____	☐	☐	☐	☐
	_____	☐	☐	☐	☐
	_____	☐	☐	☐	☐
	_____	☐	☐	☐	☐
	_____	☐	☐	☐	☐
	_____	☐	☐	☐	☐
	_____	☐	☐	☐	☐
Dining	_____	☐	☐	☐	☐
	_____	☐	☐	☐	☐
	_____	☐	☐	☐	☐
	_____	☐	☐	☐	☐
Bedrooms	_____	☐	☐	☐	☐
	_____	☐	☐	☐	☐
	_____	☐	☐	☐	☐
	_____	☐	☐	☐	☐
	_____	☐	☐	☐	☐
	_____	☐	☐	☐	☐
	_____	☐	☐	☐	☐
	_____	☐	☐	☐	☐
Kitchen	_____	☐	☐	☐	☐
	_____	☐	☐	☐	☐
	_____	☐	☐	☐	☐
	_____	☐	☐	☐	☐
	_____	☐	☐	☐	☐
Bathroom	_____	☐	☐	☐	☐
	_____	☐	☐	☐	☐
	_____	☐	☐	☐	☐
	_____	☐	☐	☐	☐
Other	_____	☐	☐	☐	☐
	_____	☐	☐	☐	☐
	_____	☐	☐	☐	☐
	_____	☐	☐	☐	☐
	_____	☐	☐	☐	☐

Gifts and Guests

GIFT REGISTRY
HOW-TO

- You and your fiancé should register your gift preferences at department and specialty stores as soon as your engagement is announced.

- By registering early, you provide a convenient way for your family and friends to select gifts for your showers and wedding.

- If your fiancé and his family are from another city, consider registering there also.

- Once you register, it is your responsibility to keep the registry current by informing the store of gifts received from other sources.

- You can eliminate confusion and save time by having an idea of those things you would like to receive as gifts before meeting with the bridal consultant.

- Record the retail price of each item on the Gift Registry list. This may be time-consuming now, but it will benefit you later when you determine the replacement value of your household furnishings for insurance purposes.

- When your wedding gifts begin arriving,

  —open each gift immediately and carefully.

  —record the gift as soon as possible or tape the card to the gift until you do.

  —if the gift arrives marred or broken, immediately call or write the store. If the giver wrapped and mailed the gift without insuring it, thank the person for it but do not mention the damage.

- It's better not to return or exchange anything before the wedding, especially if you display your gifts—some may want to see their gift.

- If you risk offending someone, it's better to keep whatever that person sent—unless you have received an exact duplicate, in which case you may safely exchange one of the gifts.

- If you choose to display your gifts, place the gifts of the same type together—all silver, all china, all linens—on tables covered with floor-length white cloths.

- To save space, you can display only one place setting of your silver, crystal, and china.

- Accompanying cards may or may not be placed with the gifts.

- For gifts of money you may receive, it is considered inappropriate to indicate the amount enclosed. You can either overlap the edges of the checks and gift certificates so only the names are visible, or recognize the gift by writing the name of the sender on a small white card with the notation: "Gift of money from _____ " or "Check from _____ " or "Gift certificate from _____."

- Gifts received at the wedding and reception are usually left unopened. You may open the gifts after the reception at the home of the bride's parents, or when you return home from your honeymoon with a small gathering of family and close friends.

- You might consider insuring your gifts with a short-term policy to cover the period of time when the gifts begin arriving until you obtain household insurance after your marriage. As a further precaution, you may want to have someone in your home during the wedding/reception festivities to protect the gifts. Usually, just having someone there is all that is needed to forestall any thievery.

GIFT REGISTRY

Fine China

Brand _____

Pattern _____

Quantity	Price	Item
_____	_____	5-pc. setting
_____	_____	Dinner plate
_____	_____	Salad plate
_____	_____	Bread/butter
_____	_____	Cup
_____	_____	Saucer
_____	_____	Soup/cereal
_____	_____	Fruit dish
_____	_____	Small platter
_____	_____	Medium platter
_____	_____	Large platter
_____	_____	Covered vegetable
_____	_____	Oval vegetable
_____	_____	Round vegetable
_____	_____	Salt/pepper
_____	_____	Butter dish
_____	_____	Gravy boat
_____	_____	Creamer
_____	_____	Sugar
_____	_____	Teapot
_____	_____	Coffeepot
_____	_____	_____
_____	_____	_____

Flatware—Formal

Brand _____

Pattern _____

Quantity	Price	Item
_____	_____	4-pc. setting
_____	_____	5-pc.—soup
_____	_____	5-pc.—2 teaspoons
_____	_____	Teaspoon
_____	_____	Salad fork
_____	_____	Fork
_____	_____	Knife
_____	_____	Place spoon
_____	_____	Iced teaspoon
_____	_____	Cocktail forks
_____	_____	Steak knives
_____	_____	Butter spreader
_____	_____	Tablespoon
_____	_____	Butter knife
_____	_____	Pierced tablespoon
_____	_____	Sugar spoon
_____	_____	Meat fork
_____	_____	Gravy ladle
_____	_____	Casserole spoon
_____	_____	Pastry server
_____	_____	Storage chest
_____	_____	_____
_____	_____	_____

Crystal

Brand _____

Pattern _____

Color _____

Quantity	Price	Item
_____	_____	Goblet
_____	_____	Wine
_____	_____	Champagne
_____	_____	Sherbet

Quantity	Price	Item
_____	_____	Cordial
_____	_____	Highball
_____	_____	Double old-fashioned
_____	_____	Decanter
_____	_____	Iced tea
_____	_____	_____
_____	_____	_____

Flatware—Casual

Brand _____

Pattern _____

Quantity	Price	Item
_____	_____	4-pc. setting
_____	_____	5-pc.—soup
_____	_____	5-pc.—2 teaspoons
_____	_____	Teaspoon
_____	_____	Salad fork
_____	_____	Fork
_____	_____	Knife
_____	_____	Place spoon
_____	_____	Iced teaspoon
_____	_____	Cocktail forks
_____	_____	Steak knives
_____	_____	Butter spreader
_____	_____	Tablespoon
_____	_____	Butter knife
_____	_____	Sugar spoon
_____	_____	Meat fork
_____	_____	Gravy ladle
_____	_____	Casserole spoon
_____	_____	Pastry server
_____	_____	Storage chest

Casual Dinnerware

Brand _____

Pattern _____

Quantity	Price	Item
_____	_____	5-pc. setting
_____	_____	5-pc. server
_____	_____	7-pc. hostess
_____	_____	20-pc. set
_____	_____	Dinner plate
_____	_____	Salad plate
_____	_____	Bread/butter
_____	_____	Cup
_____	_____	Saucer
_____	_____	Mug
_____	_____	Soup/cereal
_____	_____	Fruit dish
_____	_____	Small platter
_____	_____	Medium platter
_____	_____	Large platter

Quantity	Price	Item
_____	_____	Covered vegetable
_____	_____	Oval vegetable
_____	_____	Round vegetable
_____	_____	Salt/pepper
_____	_____	Butter dish
_____	_____	Gravy boat
_____	_____	Creamer
_____	_____	Sugar
_____	_____	Teapot
_____	_____	Coffeepot
_____	_____	
_____	_____	

Kitchen Linens

Brand _____

Pattern _____

Quantity	Price	Item
_____	_____	Apron
_____	_____	Towels
_____	_____	Pot holders/mitts
_____	_____	Place mats
_____	_____	Napkins
_____	_____	Tablecloths
_____	_____	
_____	_____	

Casual Glassware/Barware

Brand _____

Pattern _____

Color _____

Quantity	Price	Item
_____	_____	Goblet
_____	_____	Wine
_____	_____	Champagne
_____	_____	Low tumbler
_____	_____	High tumbler
_____	_____	Iced tea
_____	_____	Juice
_____	_____	Pitcher
_____	_____	24-pc. glasses set
_____	_____	Pilsner/beer glasses

Bar Equipment

Brand _____

Pattern _____

Color _____

Quantity	Price	Item
_____	_____	Ice bucket
_____	_____	Wine cooler

_____	_____	Wine rack
_____	_____	Decanter
_____	_____	Punch bowl set
_____	_____	Pitcher
_____	_____	Coasters
_____	_____	Cocktail shaker
_____	_____	_____

Cookware

Quantity	Price	Item	Brand	Style	Color
_____	_____	Saucepan—1 quart	_____	_____	_____
_____	_____	Saucepan—2 quart	_____	_____	_____
_____	_____	Saucepan—3 quart	_____	_____	_____
_____	_____	Saucepan—4 quart	_____	_____	_____
_____	_____	Double boiler	_____	_____	_____
_____	_____	Small frying pan	_____	_____	_____
_____	_____	Medium frying pan	_____	_____	_____
_____	_____	Large frying pan	_____	_____	_____
_____	_____	Stock pot	_____	_____	_____
_____	_____	Dutch oven	_____	_____	_____
_____	_____	Lasagna pan	_____	_____	_____
_____	_____	Casserole	_____	_____	_____
_____	_____	Steamer	_____	_____	_____
_____	_____	Colander	_____	_____	_____
_____	_____	Teakettle	_____	_____	_____
_____	_____	Microwave cookware	_____	_____	_____
_____	_____	Bakeware	_____	_____	_____
_____	_____	Cookie sheet	_____	_____	_____
_____	_____	Quiche dish	_____	_____	_____
_____	_____	_____	_____	_____	_____
_____	_____	_____	_____	_____	_____

Appliances

Quantity	Price	Item	Brand	Style	Color
_____	_____	Waffle maker	_____	_____	_____
_____	_____	Can opener	_____	_____	_____
_____	_____	Coffeemaker	_____	_____	_____
_____	_____	Iron	_____	_____	_____
_____	_____	Toaster	_____	_____	_____
_____	_____	Mixer (hand)	_____	_____	_____
_____	_____	Blender	_____	_____	_____
_____	_____	Slow cooker	_____	_____	_____
_____	_____	Food processor	_____	_____	_____
_____	_____	Popcorn popper	_____	_____	_____
_____	_____	Toaster oven	_____	_____	_____
_____	_____	Coffee grinder	_____	_____	_____
_____	_____	Electric wok	_____	_____	_____
_____	_____	Electric knife	_____	_____	_____
_____	_____	Electric juicer	_____	_____	_____
_____	_____	Ice cream maker	_____	_____	_____
_____	_____	Pasta machine	_____	_____	_____
_____	_____	Broiler/rotisserie	_____	_____	_____
_____	_____	Fondue pot	_____	_____	_____
_____	_____	Convection oven	_____	_____	_____
_____	_____	Clock	_____	_____	_____
_____	_____	Vacuum cleaner	_____	_____	_____
_____	_____	Espresso machine	_____	_____	_____
_____	_____	Microwave oven	_____	_____	_____
_____	_____	_____	_____	_____	_____
_____	_____	_____	_____	_____	_____
_____	_____	_____	_____	_____	_____
_____	_____	_____	_____	_____	_____

Kitchenware

Quantity	Price	Item	Brand	Style	Color
_____	_____	Ironing board	_____	_____	_____
_____	_____	Cutlery	_____	_____	_____
_____	_____	Steak knives	_____	_____	_____
_____	_____	Cutting board	_____	_____	_____
_____	_____	Utensil set	_____	_____	_____
_____	_____	Mixing bowls	_____	_____	_____
_____	_____	Canister set	_____	_____	_____
_____	_____	Spice rack	_____	_____	_____
_____	_____	Cookbooks	_____	_____	_____
_____	_____	Measuring cups	_____	_____	_____
_____	_____	Jell-O molds	_____	_____	_____
_____	_____	Oven timer	_____	_____	_____
_____	_____	Storage containers	_____	_____	_____
_____	_____	Thermometer	_____	_____	_____
_____	_____	_____	_____	_____	_____
_____	_____	_____	_____	_____	_____

Serving Dishes/Table Accessories

Quantity	Price	Item	Brand	Style	Color
_____	_____	Salt and pepper	_____	_____	_____
_____	_____	Platter	_____	_____	_____
_____	_____	Gravy boat	_____	_____	_____
_____	_____	Bread tray	_____	_____	_____
_____	_____	Vegetable dish	_____	_____	_____
_____	_____	Covered casserole	_____	_____	_____
_____	_____	Chafing dish	_____	_____	_____
_____	_____	Salad bowl	_____	_____	_____
_____	_____	Salad server	_____	_____	_____
_____	_____	Butter dish	_____	_____	_____
_____	_____	Relish dish	_____	_____	_____

		Chip-and-dip bowl _____		_____	_____
_____	_____	Pitcher	_____	_____	_____
_____	_____	Serving tray	_____	_____	_____
_____	_____	Sugar and creamer	_____	_____	_____
_____	_____	Coffee/tea set	_____	_____	_____
_____	_____	Compote dish	_____	_____	_____
_____	_____	Candlesticks (pair) _____		_____	_____
_____	_____	Napkin rings	_____	_____	_____
_____	_____	_____	_____	_____	_____
_____	_____	_____	_____	_____	_____

Bedroom Linens—Bedroom #1

(bed size: _____)

QUANTITY	PRICE	ITEM	BRAND	STYLE	COLOR
_____	_____	Flat sheets	_____	_____	_____
_____	_____	Flat sheets	_____	_____	_____
_____	_____	Fitted sheets	_____	_____	_____
_____	_____	Fitted sheets	_____	_____	_____
_____	_____	Pillowcases	_____	_____	_____
_____	_____	Pillowcases	_____	_____	_____
_____	_____	Pillows	_____	_____	_____
_____	_____	Blanket, lightweight _____		_____	_____
_____	_____	Blanket, woolen	_____	_____	_____
_____	_____	Electric blanket	_____	_____	_____
_____	_____	Bedspread	_____	_____	_____
_____	_____	Comforter/quilt	_____	_____	_____
_____	_____	Pillow shams	_____	_____	_____
_____	_____	Dust ruffle	_____	_____	_____
_____	_____	Mattress pad	_____	_____	_____
_____	_____	Pillow protector	_____	_____	_____
_____	_____	_____	_____	_____	_____
_____	_____	_____	_____	_____	_____

Bedroom Linens—Bedroom #2

(bed size: _____)

Quantity	Price	Item	Brand	Style	Color
_____	_____	Flat sheets	_____	_____	_____
_____	_____	Flat sheets	_____	_____	_____
_____	_____	Fitted sheets	_____	_____	_____
_____	_____	Fitted sheets	_____	_____	_____
_____	_____	Pillowcases	_____	_____	_____
_____	_____	Pillowcases	_____	_____	_____
_____	_____	Pillows	_____	_____	_____
_____	_____	Blanket, lightweight	_____	_____	_____
_____	_____	Blanket, woolen	_____	_____	_____
_____	_____	Electric blanket	_____	_____	_____
_____	_____	Bedspread	_____	_____	_____
_____	_____	Comforter/quilt	_____	_____	_____
_____	_____	Pillow shams	_____	_____	_____
_____	_____	Dust ruffle	_____	_____	_____
_____	_____	Mattress pad	_____	_____	_____
_____	_____	Pillow protector	_____	_____	_____
_____	_____	_____	_____	_____	_____
_____	_____	_____	_____	_____	_____
_____	_____	_____	_____	_____	_____

Bath #1

Quantity	Price	Item	Brand	Style	Color
_____	_____	Bath towels	_____	_____	_____
_____	_____	Bath towels	_____	_____	_____
_____	_____	Hand towels	_____	_____	_____
_____	_____	Hand towels	_____	_____	_____
_____	_____	Washcloths	_____	_____	_____
_____	_____	Washcloths	_____	_____	_____
_____	_____	Fingertip towels	_____	_____	_____

		Fingertip towels			
———	———	Bath sheets	———	———	———
———	———	Bath rug	———	———	———
———	———	Contour rug	———	———	———
———	———	Lid cover	———	———	———
———	———	Bath mat	———	———	———
———	———	Shower curtain	———	———	———
———	———	Tissue holder	———	———	———
———	———	Tumbler/soap dish	———	———	———
———	———	Wastebasket	———	———	———
———	———	Hamper	———	———	———
———	———	Pool towels	———	———	———
———	———	Tank set	———	———	———
———	———	———————	———	———	———
———	———	———————	———	———	———

Bath #2

Quantity	Price	Item	Brand	Style	Color
———	———	Bath towels	———	———	———
———	———	Bath towels	———	———	———
———	———	Hand towels	———	———	———
———	———	Hand towels	———	———	———
———	———	Washcloths	———	———	———
———	———	Washcloths	———	———	———
———	———	Fingertip towels	———	———	———
———	———	Fingertip towels	———	———	———
———	———	Bath sheets	———	———	———
———	———	Bath rug	———	———	———
———	———	Contour rug	———	———	———
———	———	Lid cover	———	———	———
———	———	Bath mat	———	———	———
———	———	Shower curtain	———	———	———

		Tissue holder	_____	_____	_____
_____	_____	Tumbler/soap dish	_____	_____	_____
_____	_____	Wastebasket	_____	_____	_____
_____	_____	Hamper	_____	_____	_____
_____	_____	Pool towels	_____	_____	_____
_____	_____	Tank set	_____	_____	_____
_____	_____	_____	_____	_____	_____
_____	_____	_____	_____	_____	_____

Electronics

Quantity	Price	Item	Brand	Style	Color
_____	_____	Television	_____	_____	_____
_____	_____	VCR	_____	_____	_____
_____	_____	Clock/radio	_____	_____	_____
_____	_____	Stereo system	_____	_____	_____
_____	_____	_____	_____	_____	_____
_____	_____	_____	_____	_____	_____
_____	_____	_____	_____	_____	_____

Specialty Items

Quantity	Price	Item	Brand	Style	Color
_____	_____	Luggage	_____	_____	_____
_____	_____	Exercise equipment	_____	_____	_____
_____	_____	Camping gear	_____	_____	_____
_____	_____	Tools	_____	_____	_____
_____	_____	_____	_____	_____	_____
_____	_____	_____	_____	_____	_____
_____	_____	_____	_____	_____	_____

Gift Registry Locations

#1	#2	#3
Name _____	Name _____	Name _____
_____	_____	_____
Address _____	Address _____	Address _____
_____	_____	_____
Contact person _____	Contact person _____	Contact person _____
_____	_____	_____
Phone _____	Phone _____	Phone _____
_____	_____	_____

GUEST LIST HOW-TO

- The size of your guest list will be determined by your budget and by the size of your ceremony and reception sites.

- The list may be divided with one-half of the guests for each family or it can be divided into thirds: one-third for each family and one-third for the bridal couple.

- Generally only 65 to 85 percent of the invited people attend. The number attending depends on several factors: the time of day, time of year, day of week, and the social or professional prominence of the bridal couple and their parents.

- State a limit to each family before they begin compiling their lists. It's much easier to add names after the list has been formed than to have to delete names.

- Set a deadline with your families for giving you the names on their lists.

- Unless it causes a family problem, invite only those you truly want to share your day. This should not be a time for repaying professional or social debts.

- You will need complete names and addresses for addressing the invitations, including names of any children to be invited.

- Phone numbers are helpful if you need to contact any late respondents.

- You may want to alphabetize the names in the Guest List. If so, set aside the approximate number of pages that you will need for each letter or letter combinations.

- Use the boxes on the Guest List next to the name to number your list. This number can be lightly written on the back of the corresponding response card before you send your invitations. When the card is returned from the guest, match the number on the card to the name on the list—a helpful system for guests with illegible handwriting.

- Knowing the number of guests actually planning to attend is important—it will determine the cost of your reception. The caterer will take your word for the number of guests and charge you accordingly.

- Your confirmation total could reflect the additional number of guests that most caterers are prepared to serve the day of the wedding. This allows for people who at the last moment are unable to attend. Ask if your caterer is willing to share this number with you.

- If some have failed to reply by a week before the wedding and you are uncertain of their plans, call them for a response. Your mother, your future mother-in-law, or friends can help you with the calling.

- Everyone invited to the wedding ceremony needs to be invited to the reception, but you may invite more people to the reception than to the ceremony.

- Announcement cards can be sent to those who cannot attend, whether they live too far away or the wedding and reception sites are too small to accommodate them.

GUEST LIST

❑Name: _____ Phone: _____ Gifts   Thank You
Children:_____ Shower: _____ ❑
Address:_____ Shower: _____ ❑
City: _____ State: _____ Zip: _____ Wedding:_____ ❑
Wedding Invitation: ❑ Reception Invitation: ❑ Announcements: ❑ RSVP: Yes ❑ No ❑ Number Invited _____ Number Attending _____

❑Name: _____ Phone: _____ Gifts   Thank You
Children:_____ Shower: _____ ❑
Address:_____ Shower: _____ ❑
City: _____ State: _____ Zip: _____ Wedding:_____ ❑
Wedding Invitation: ❑ Reception Invitation: ❑ Announcements: ❑ RSVP: Yes ❑ No ❑ Number Invited _____ Number Attending _____

❑Name: _____ Phone: _____ Gifts   Thank You
Children:_____ Shower: _____ ❑
Address:_____ Shower: _____ ❑
City: _____ State: _____ Zip: _____ Wedding:_____ ❑
Wedding Invitation: ❑ Reception Invitation: ❑ Announcements: ❑ RSVP: Yes ❑ No ❑ Number Invited _____ Number Attending _____

❑Name: _____ Phone: _____ Gifts   Thank You
Children:_____ Shower: _____ ❑
Address:_____ Shower: _____ ❑
City: _____ State: _____ Zip: _____ Wedding:_____ ❑
Wedding Invitation: ❑ Reception Invitation: ❑ Announcements: ❑ RSVP: Yes ❑ No ❑ Number Invited _____ Number Attending _____

❑Name: _____ Phone: _____ Gifts   Thank You
Children:_____ Shower: _____ ❑
Address:_____ Shower: _____ ❑
City: _____ State: _____ Zip: _____ Wedding:_____ ❑
Wedding Invitation: ❑ Reception Invitation: ❑ Announcements: ❑ RSVP: Yes ❑ No ❑ Number Invited _____ Number Attending _____

❑Name: _____ Phone: _____ Gifts   Thank You
Children:_____ Shower: _____ ❑
Address:_____ Shower: _____ ❑
City: _____ State: _____ Zip: _____ Wedding:_____ ❑
Wedding Invitation: ❑ Reception Invitation: ❑ Announcements: ❑ RSVP: Yes ❑ No ❑ Number Invited _____ Number Attending _____

❑Name: _____ Phone: _____ Gifts   Thank You
Children:_____ Shower: _____ ❑
Address:_____ Shower: _____ ❑
City: _____ State: _____ Zip: _____ Wedding:_____ ❑
Wedding Invitation: ❑ Reception Invitation: ❑ Announcements: ❑ RSVP: Yes ❑ No ❑ Number Invited _____ Number Attending _____

Name: _____ Phone: _____ Gifts   Thank You
Children:_____ Shower: _____ ❑
Address:_____ Shower: _____ ❑
City: _____ State: _____ Zip: _____ Wedding:_____ ❑
Wedding Invitation: ❑ Reception Invitation: ❑ Announcements: ❑ RSVP: Yes ❑ No ❑ Number Invited _____ Number Attending _____

❑Name: _____ Phone: _____ Gifts   Thank You
Children:_____ Shower: _____ ❑
Address:_____ Shower: _____ ❑
City: _____ State: _____ Zip: _____ Wedding:_____ ❑
Wedding Invitation: ❑ Reception Invitation: ❑ Announcements: ❑ RSVP: Yes ❑ No ❑ Number Invited _____ Number Attending _____

❑Name: _____ Phone: _____ Gifts   Thank You
Children:_____ Shower: _____ ❑
Address:_____ Shower: _____ ❑
City: _____ State: _____ Zip: _____ Wedding:_____ ❑
Wedding Invitation: ❑ Reception Invitation: ❑ Announcements: ❑ RSVP: Yes ❑ No ❑ Number Invited _____ Number Attending _____

❑Name: _____ Phone: _____ Gifts   Thank You
Children:_____ Shower: _____ ❑
Address:_____ Shower: _____ ❑
City: _____ State: _____ Zip: _____ Wedding:_____ ❑
Wedding Invitation: ❑ Reception Invitation: ❑ Announcements: ❑ RSVP: Yes ❑ No ❑ Number Invited _____ Number Attending _____

❑Name: _____ Phone: _____ Gifts   Thank You
Children:_____ Shower: _____ ❑
Address:_____ Shower: _____ ❑
City: _____ State: _____ Zip: _____ Wedding:_____ ❑
Wedding Invitation: ❑ Reception Invitation: ❑ Announcements: ❑ RSVP: Yes ❑ No ❑ Number Invited _____ Number Attending _____
❑Name: _____ Phone: _____ Gifts   Thank You
Children:_____ Shower: _____ ❑
Address:_____ Shower: _____ ❑
City: _____ State: _____ Zip: _____ Wedding:_____ ❑
Wedding Invitation: ❑ Reception Invitation: ❑ Announcements: ❑ RSVP: Yes ❑ No ❑ Number Invited _____ Number Attending _____
❑Name: _____ Phone: _____ Gifts   Thank You
Children:_____ Shower: _____ ❑
Address:_____ Shower: _____ ❑
City: _____ State: _____ Zip: _____ Wedding:_____ ❑
Wedding Invitation: ❑ Reception Invitation: ❑ Announcements: ❑ RSVP: Yes ❑ No ❑ Number Invited _____ Number Attending _____
❑Name: _____ Phone: _____ Gifts   Thank You
Children:_____ Shower: _____ ❑
Address:_____ Shower: _____ ❑
City: _____ State: _____ Zip: _____ Wedding:_____ ❑
Wedding Invitation: ❑ Reception Invitation: ❑ Announcements: ❑ RSVP: Yes ❑ No ❑ Number Invited _____ Number Attending _____
❑Name: _____ Phone: _____ Gifts   Thank You
Children:_____ Shower: _____ ❑
Address:_____ Shower: _____ ❑
City: _____ State: _____ Zip: _____ Wedding:_____ ❑
Wedding Invitation: ❑ Reception Invitation: ❑ Announcements: ❑ RSVP: Yes ❑ No ❑ Number Invited _____ Number Attending _____
❑Name: _____ Phone: _____ Gifts   Thank You
Children:_____ Shower: _____ ❑
Address:_____ Shower: _____ ❑
City: _____ State: _____ Zip: _____ Wedding:_____ ❑
Wedding Invitation: ❑ Reception Invitation: ❑ Announcements: ❑ RSVP: Yes ❑ No ❑ Number Invited _____ Number Attending _____
❑Name: _____ Phone: _____ Gifts   Thank You
Children:_____ Shower: _____ ❑
Address:_____ Shower: _____ ❑
City: _____ State: _____ Zip: _____ Wedding:_____ ❑
Wedding Invitation: ❑ Reception Invitation: ❑ Announcements: ❑ RSVP: Yes ❑ No ❑ Number Invited _____ Number Attending _____
Name: _____ Phone: _____ Gifts   Thank You
Children:_____ Shower: _____ ❑
Address:_____ Shower: _____ ❑
City: _____ State: _____ Zip: _____ Wedding:_____ ❑
Wedding Invitation: ❑ Reception Invitation: ❑ Announcements: ❑ RSVP: Yes ❑ No ❑ Number Invited _____ Number Attending _____
❑Name: _____ Phone: _____ Gifts   Thank You
Children:_____ Shower: _____ ❑
Address:_____ Shower: _____ ❑
City: _____ State: _____ Zip: _____ Wedding:_____ ❑
Wedding Invitation: ❑ Reception Invitation: ❑ Announcements: ❑ RSVP: Yes ❑ No ❑ Number Invited _____ Number Attending _____
❑Name: _____ Phone: _____ Gifts   Thank You
Children:_____ Shower: _____ ❑
Address:_____ Shower: _____ ❑
City: _____ State: _____ Zip: _____ Wedding:_____ ❑
Wedding Invitation: ❑ Reception Invitation: ❑ Announcements: ❑ RSVP: Yes ❑ No ❑ Number Invited _____ Number Attending _____
❑Name: _____ Phone: _____ Gifts   Thank You
Children:_____ Shower: _____ ❑
Address:_____ Shower: _____ ❑
City: _____ State: _____ Zip: _____ Wedding:_____ ❑
Wedding Invitation: ❑ Reception Invitation: ❑ Announcements: ❑ RSVP: Yes ❑ No ❑ Number Invited _____ Number Attending _____

❏Name: _____ Phone: _____ Gifts   Thank You
Children:_____ Shower: _____ ❏
Address:_____ Shower: _____ ❏
City: _____ State: _____ Zip: _____ Wedding:_____ ❏
Wedding Invitation: ❏ Reception Invitation: ❏ Announcements: ❏ RSVP: Yes ❏ No ❏ Number Invited ____ Number Attending ____

❏Name: _____ Phone: _____ Gifts   Thank You
Children:_____ Shower: _____ ❏
Address:_____ Shower: _____ ❏
City: _____ State: _____ Zip: _____ Wedding:_____ ❏
Wedding Invitation: ❏ Reception Invitation: ❏ Announcements: ❏ RSVP: Yes ❏ No ❏ Number Invited ____ Number Attending ____

❏Name: _____ Phone: _____ Gifts   Thank You
Children:_____ Shower: _____ ❏
Address:_____ Shower: _____ ❏
City: _____ State: _____ Zip: _____ Wedding:_____ ❏
Wedding Invitation: ❏ Reception Invitation: ❏ Announcements: ❏ RSVP: Yes ❏ No ❏ Number Invited ____ Number Attending ____

❏Name: _____ Phone: _____ Gifts   Thank You
Children:_____ Shower: _____ ❏
Address:_____ Shower: _____ ❏
City: _____ State: _____ Zip: _____ Wedding:_____ ❏
Wedding Invitation: ❏ Reception Invitation: ❏ Announcements: ❏ RSVP: Yes ❏ No ❏ Number Invited ____ Number Attending ____

❏Name: _____ Phone: _____ Gifts   Thank You
Children:_____ Shower: _____ ❏
Address:_____ Shower: _____ ❏
City: _____ State: _____ Zip: _____ Wedding:_____ ❏
Wedding Invitation: ❏ Reception Invitation: ❏ Announcements: ❏ RSVP: Yes ❏ No ❏ Number Invited ____ Number Attending ____

❏Name: _____ Phone: _____ Gifts   Thank You
Children:_____ Shower: _____ ❏
Address:_____ Shower: _____ ❏
City: _____ State: _____ Zip: _____ Wedding:_____ ❏
Wedding Invitation: ❏ Reception Invitation: ❏ Announcements: ❏ RSVP: Yes ❏ No ❏ Number Invited ____ Number Attending ____

❏Name: _____ Phone: _____ Gifts   Thank You
Children:_____ Shower: _____ ❏
Address:_____ Shower: _____ ❏
City: _____ State: _____ Zip: _____ Wedding:_____ ❏
Wedding Invitation: ❏ Reception Invitation: ❏ Announcements: ❏ RSVP: Yes ❏ No ❏ Number Invited ____ Number Attending ____

Name: _____ Phone: _____ Gifts   Thank You
Children:_____ Shower: _____ ❏
Address:_____ Shower: _____ ❏
City: _____ State: _____ Zip: _____ Wedding:_____ ❏
Wedding Invitation: ❏ Reception Invitation: ❏ Announcements: ❏ RSVP: Yes ❏ No ❏ Number Invited ____ Number Attending ____

❏Name: _____ Phone: _____ Gifts   Thank You
Children:_____ Shower: _____ ❏
Address:_____ Shower: _____ ❏
City: _____ State: _____ Zip: _____ Wedding:_____ ❏
Wedding Invitation: ❏ Reception Invitation: ❏ Announcements: ❏ RSVP: Yes ❏ No ❏ Number Invited ____ Number Attending ____

❏Name: _____ Phone: _____ Gifts   Thank You
Children:_____ Shower: _____ ❏
Address:_____ Shower: _____ ❏
City: _____ State: _____ Zip: _____ Wedding:_____ ❏
Wedding Invitation: ❏ Reception Invitation: ❏ Announcements: ❏ RSVP: Yes ❏ No ❏ Number Invited ____ Number Attending ____

❏Name: _____ Phone: _____ Gifts   Thank You
Children:_____ Shower: _____ ❏
Address:_____ Shower: _____ ❏
City: _____ State: _____ Zip: _____ Wedding:_____ ❏
Wedding Invitation: ❏ Reception Invitation: ❏ Announcements: ❏ RSVP: Yes ❏ No ❏ Number Invited ____ Number Attending ____

❏Name: _____ Phone: _____ Gifts   Thank You
Children:_____ Shower: _____ ❏
Address:_____ Shower: _____ ❏
City: _____ State: _____ Zip: _____ Wedding:_____ ❏
Wedding Invitation: ❏ Reception Invitation: ❏ Announcements: ❏ RSVP: Yes ❏ No ❏ Number Invited _____ Number Attending _____

❏Name: _____ Phone: _____ Gifts   Thank You
Children:_____ Shower: _____ ❏
Address:_____ Shower: _____ ❏
City: _____ State: _____ Zip: _____ Wedding:_____ ❏
Wedding Invitation: ❏ Reception Invitation: ❏ Announcements: ❏ RSVP: Yes ❏ No ❏ Number Invited _____ Number Attending _____

❏Name: _____ Phone: _____ Gifts   Thank You
Children:_____ Shower: _____ ❏
Address:_____ Shower: _____ ❏
City: _____ State: _____ Zip: _____ Wedding:_____ ❏
Wedding Invitation: ❏ Reception Invitation: ❏ Announcements: ❏ RSVP: Yes ❏ No ❏ Number Invited _____ Number Attending _____

❏Name: _____ Phone: _____ Gifts   Thank You
Children:_____ Shower: _____ ❏
Address:_____ Shower: _____ ❏
City: _____ State: _____ Zip: _____ Wedding:_____ ❏
Wedding Invitation: ❏ Reception Invitation: ❏ Announcements: ❏ RSVP: Yes ❏ No ❏ Number Invited _____ Number Attending _____

❏Name: _____ Phone: _____ Gifts   Thank You
Children:_____ Shower: _____ ❏
Address:_____ Shower: _____ ❏
City: _____ State: _____ Zip: _____ Wedding:_____ ❏
Wedding Invitation: ❏ Reception Invitation: ❏ Announcements: ❏ RSVP: Yes ❏ No ❏ Number Invited _____ Number Attending _____

❏Name: _____ Phone: _____ Gifts   Thank You
Children:_____ Shower: _____ ❏
Address:_____ Shower: _____ ❏
City: _____ State: _____ Zip: _____ Wedding:_____ ❏
Wedding Invitation: ❏ Reception Invitation: ❏ Announcements: ❏ RSVP: Yes ❏ No ❏ Number Invited _____ Number Attending _____

❏Name: _____ Phone: _____ Gifts   Thank You
Children:_____ Shower: _____ ❏
Address:_____ Shower: _____ ❏
City: _____ State: _____ Zip: _____ Wedding:_____ ❏
Wedding Invitation: ❏ Reception Invitation: ❏ Announcements: ❏ RSVP: Yes ❏ No ❏ Number Invited _____ Number Attending _____

Name: _____ Phone: _____ Gifts   Thank You
Children:_____ Shower: _____ ❏
Address:_____ Shower: _____ ❏
City: _____ State: _____ Zip: _____ Wedding:_____ ❏
Wedding Invitation: ❏ Reception Invitation: ❏ Announcements: ❏ RSVP: Yes ❏ No ❏ Number Invited _____ Number Attending _____

❏Name: _____ Phone: _____ Gifts   Thank You
Children:_____ Shower: _____ ❏
Address:_____ Shower: _____ ❏
City: _____ State: _____ Zip: _____ Wedding:_____ ❏
Wedding Invitation: ❏ Reception Invitation: ❏ Announcements: ❏ RSVP: Yes ❏ No ❏ Number Invited _____ Number Attending _____

❏Name: _____ Phone: _____ Gifts   Thank You
Children:_____ Shower: _____ ❏
Address:_____ Shower: _____ ❏
City: _____ State: _____ Zip: _____ Wedding:_____ ❏
Wedding Invitation: ❏ Reception Invitation: ❏ Announcements: ❏ RSVP: Yes ❏ No ❏ Number Invited _____ Number Attending _____

❏Name: _____ Phone: _____ Gifts   Thank You
Children:_____ Shower: _____ ❏
Address:_____ Shower: _____ ❏
City: _____ State: _____ Zip: _____ Wedding:_____ ❏
Wedding Invitation: ❏ Reception Invitation: ❏ Announcements: ❏ RSVP: Yes ❏ No ❏ Number Invited _____ Number Attending _____

❏Name: _____ Phone: _____ Gifts   Thank You
Children:_____ Shower: _____ ❏
Address:_____ Shower: _____ ❏
City: _____ State: _____ Zip: _____ Wedding:_____ ❏
Wedding Invitation: ❏ Reception Invitation: ❏ Announcements: ❏ RSVP: Yes ❏ No ❏ Number Invited _____ Number Attending _____

❏Name: _____ Phone: _____ Gifts   Thank You
Children:_____ Shower: _____ ❏
Address:_____ Shower: _____ ❏
City: _____ State: _____ Zip: _____ Wedding:_____ ❏
Wedding Invitation: ❏ Reception Invitation: ❏ Announcements: ❏ RSVP: Yes ❏ No ❏ Number Invited _____ Number Attending _____

❏Name: _____ Phone: _____ Gifts   Thank You
Children:_____ Shower: _____ ❏
Address:_____ Shower: _____ ❏
City: _____ State: _____ Zip: _____ Wedding:_____ ❏
Wedding Invitation: ❏ Reception Invitation: ❏ Announcements: ❏ RSVP: Yes ❏ No ❏ Number Invited _____ Number Attending _____

❏Name: _____ Phone: _____ Gifts   Thank You
Children:_____ Shower: _____ ❏
Address:_____ Shower: _____ ❏
City: _____ State: _____ Zip: _____ Wedding:_____ ❏
Wedding Invitation: ❏ Reception Invitation: ❏ Announcements: ❏ RSVP: Yes ❏ No ❏ Number Invited _____ Number Attending _____

❏Name: _____ Phone: _____ Gifts   Thank You
Children:_____ Shower: _____ ❏
Address:_____ Shower: _____ ❏
City: _____ State: _____ Zip: _____ Wedding:_____ ❏
Wedding Invitation: ❏ Reception Invitation: ❏ Announcements: ❏ RSVP: Yes ❏ No ❏ Number Invited _____ Number Attending _____

❏Name: _____ Phone: _____ Gifts   Thank You
Children:_____ Shower: _____ ❏
Address:_____ Shower: _____ ❏
City: _____ State: _____ Zip: _____ Wedding:_____ ❏
Wedding Invitation: ❏ Reception Invitation: ❏ Announcements: ❏ RSVP: Yes ❏ No ❏ Number Invited _____ Number Attending _____

❏Name: _____ Phone: _____ Gifts   Thank You
Children:_____ Shower: _____ ❏
Address:_____ Shower: _____ ❏
City: _____ State: _____ Zip: _____ Wedding:_____ ❏
Wedding Invitation: ❏ Reception Invitation: ❏ Announcements: ❏ RSVP: Yes ❏ No ❏ Number Invited _____ Number Attending _____

Name: _____ Phone: _____ Gifts   Thank You
Children:_____ Shower: _____ ❏
Address:_____ Shower: _____ ❏
City: _____ State: _____ Zip: _____ Wedding:_____ ❏
Wedding Invitation: ❏ Reception Invitation: ❏ Announcements: ❏ RSVP: Yes ❏ No ❏ Number Invited _____ Number Attending _____

❏Name: _____ Phone: _____ Gifts   Thank You
Children:_____ Shower: _____ ❏
Address:_____ Shower: _____ ❏
City: _____ State: _____ Zip: _____ Wedding:_____ ❏
Wedding Invitation: ❏ Reception Invitation: ❏ Announcements: ❏ RSVP: Yes ❏ No ❏ Number Invited _____ Number Attending _____

❏Name: _____ Phone: _____ Gifts   Thank You
Children:_____ Shower: _____ ❏
Address:_____ Shower: _____ ❏
City: _____ State: _____ Zip: _____ Wedding:_____ ❏
Wedding Invitation: ❏ Reception Invitation: ❏ Announcements: ❏ RSVP: Yes ❏ No ❏ Number Invited _____ Number Attending _____

❏Name: _____ Phone: _____ Gifts   Thank You
Children:_____ Shower: _____ ❏
Address:_____ Shower: _____ ❏
City: _____ State: _____ Zip: _____ Wedding:_____ ❏
Wedding Invitation: ❏ Reception Invitation: ❏ Announcements: ❏ RSVP: Yes ❏ No ❏ Number Invited _____ Number Attending _____

❏Name: _____ Phone: _____ Gifts .... Thank You
Children:_____ Shower: _____ ❏
Address:_____ Shower: _____ ❏
City: _____ State: _____ Zip: _____ Wedding:_____ ❏
Wedding Invitation: ❏ Reception Invitation: ❏ Announcements: ❏ RSVP: Yes ❏ No ❏ Number Invited ____ Number Attending ____

❏Name: _____ Phone: _____ Gifts .... Thank You
Children:_____ Shower: _____ ❏
Address:_____ Shower: _____ ❏
City: _____ State: _____ Zip: _____ Wedding:_____ ❏
Wedding Invitation: ❏ Reception Invitation: ❏ Announcements: ❏ RSVP: Yes ❏ No ❏ Number Invited ____ Number Attending ____

❏Name: _____ Phone: _____ Gifts .... Thank You
Children:_____ Shower: _____ ❏
Address:_____ Shower: _____ ❏
City: _____ State: _____ Zip: _____ Wedding:_____ ❏
Wedding Invitation: ❏ Reception Invitation: ❏ Announcements: ❏ RSVP: Yes ❏ No ❏ Number Invited ____ Number Attending ____

❏Name: _____ Phone: _____ Gifts .... Thank You
Children:_____ Shower: _____ ❏
Address:_____ Shower: _____ ❏
City: _____ State: _____ Zip: _____ Wedding:_____ ❏
Wedding Invitation: ❏ Reception Invitation: ❏ Announcements: ❏ RSVP: Yes ❏ No ❏ Number Invited ____ Number Attending ____

❏Name: _____ Phone: _____ Gifts .... Thank You
Children:_____ Shower: _____ ❏
Address:_____ Shower: _____ ❏
City: _____ State: _____ Zip: _____ Wedding:_____ ❏
Wedding Invitation: ❏ Reception Invitation: ❏ Announcements: ❏ RSVP: Yes ❏ No ❏ Number Invited ____ Number Attending ____

❏Name: _____ Phone: _____ Gifts .... Thank You
Children:_____ Shower: _____ ❏
Address:_____ Shower: _____ ❏
City: _____ State: _____ Zip: _____ Wedding:_____ ❏
Wedding Invitation: ❏ Reception Invitation: ❏ Announcements: ❏ RSVP: Yes ❏ No ❏ Number Invited ____ Number Attending ____

❏Name: _____ Phone: _____ Gifts .... Thank You
Children:_____ Shower: _____ ❏
Address:_____ Shower: _____ ❏
City: _____ State: _____ Zip: _____ Wedding:_____ ❏
Wedding Invitation: ❏ Reception Invitation: ❏ Announcements: ❏ RSVP: Yes ❏ No ❏ Number Invited ____ Number Attending ____

Name: _____ Phone: _____ Gifts .... Thank You
Children:_____ Shower: _____ ❏
Address:_____ Shower: _____ ❏
City: _____ State: _____ Zip: _____ Wedding:_____ ❏
Wedding Invitation: ❏ Reception Invitation: ❏ Announcements: ❏ RSVP: Yes ❏ No ❏ Number Invited ____ Number Attending ____

❏Name: _____ Phone: _____ Gifts .... Thank You
Children:_____ Shower: _____ ❏
Address:_____ Shower: _____ ❏
City: _____ State: _____ Zip: _____ Wedding:_____ ❏
Wedding Invitation: ❏ Reception Invitation: ❏ Announcements: ❏ RSVP: Yes ❏ No ❏ Number Invited ____ Number Attending ____

❏Name: _____ Phone: _____ Gifts .... Thank You
Children:_____ Shower: _____ ❏
Address:_____ Shower: _____ ❏
City: _____ State: _____ Zip: _____ Wedding:_____ ❏
Wedding Invitation: ❏ Reception Invitation: ❏ Announcements: ❏ RSVP: Yes ❏ No ❏ Number Invited ____ Number Attending ____

❏Name: _____ Phone: _____ Gifts .... Thank You
Children:_____ Shower: _____ ❏
Address:_____ Shower: _____ ❏
City: _____ State: _____ Zip: _____ Wedding:_____ ❏
Wedding Invitation: ❏ Reception Invitation: ❏ Announcements: ❏ RSVP: Yes ❏ No ❏ Number Invited ____ Number Attending ____

❏Name: _____ Phone: _____ Gifts   Thank You
Children:_____ Shower: _____ ❏
Address:_____ Shower: _____ ❏
City: _____ State: _____ Zip: _____ Wedding:_____ ❏
Wedding Invitation: ❏ Reception Invitation: ❏ Announcements: ❏ RSVP: Yes ❏ No ❏ Number Invited _____ Number Attending _____

❏Name: _____ Phone: _____ Gifts   Thank You
Children:_____ Shower: _____ ❏
Address:_____ Shower: _____ ❏
City: _____ State: _____ Zip: _____ Wedding:_____ ❏
Wedding Invitation: ❏ Reception Invitation: ❏ Announcements: ❏ RSVP: Yes ❏ No ❏ Number Invited _____ Number Attending _____

❏Name: _____ Phone: _____ Gifts   Thank You
Children:_____ Shower: _____ ❏
Address:_____ Shower: _____ ❏
City: _____ State: _____ Zip: _____ Wedding:_____ ❏
Wedding Invitation: ❏ Reception Invitation: ❏ Announcements: ❏ RSVP: Yes ❏ No ❏ Number Invited _____ Number Attending _____

❏Name: _____ Phone: _____ Gifts   Thank You
Children:_____ Shower: _____ ❏
Address:_____ Shower: _____ ❏
City: _____ State: _____ Zip: _____ Wedding:_____ ❏
Wedding Invitation: ❏ Reception Invitation: ❏ Announcements: ❏ RSVP: Yes ❏ No ❏ Number Invited _____ Number Attending _____

❏Name: _____ Phone: _____ Gifts   Thank You
Children:_____ Shower: _____ ❏
Address:_____ Shower: _____ ❏
City: _____ State: _____ Zip: _____ Wedding:_____ ❏
Wedding Invitation: ❏ Reception Invitation: ❏ Announcements: ❏ RSVP: Yes ❏ No ❏ Number Invited _____ Number Attending _____

❏Name: _____ Phone: _____ Gifts   Thank You
Children:_____ Shower: _____ ❏
Address:_____ Shower: _____ ❏
City: _____ State: _____ Zip: _____ Wedding:_____ ❏
Wedding Invitation: ❏ Reception Invitation: ❏ Announcements: ❏ RSVP: Yes ❏ No ❏ Number Invited _____ Number Attending _____

❏Name: _____ Phone: _____ Gifts   Thank You
Children:_____ Shower: _____ ❏
Address:_____ Shower: _____ ❏
City: _____ State: _____ Zip: _____ Wedding:_____ ❏
Wedding Invitation: ❏ Reception Invitation: ❏ Announcements: ❏ RSVP: Yes ❏ No ❏ Number Invited _____ Number Attending _____

Name: _____ Phone: _____ Gifts   Thank You
Children:_____ Shower: _____ ❏
Address:_____ Shower: _____ ❏
City: _____ State: _____ Zip: _____ Wedding:_____ ❏
Wedding Invitation: ❏ Reception Invitation: ❏ Announcements: ❏ RSVP: Yes ❏ No ❏ Number Invited _____ Number Attending _____

❏Name: _____ Phone: _____ Gifts   Thank You
Children:_____ Shower: _____ ❏
Address:_____ Shower: _____ ❏
City: _____ State: _____ Zip: _____ Wedding:_____ ❏
Wedding Invitation: ❏ Reception Invitation: ❏ Announcements: ❏ RSVP: Yes ❏ No ❏ Number Invited _____ Number Attending _____

❏Name: _____ Phone: _____ Gifts   Thank You
Children:_____ Shower: _____ ❏
Address:_____ Shower: _____ ❏
City: _____ State: _____ Zip: _____ Wedding:_____ ❏
Wedding Invitation: ❏ Reception Invitation: ❏ Announcements: ❏ RSVP: Yes ❏ No ❏ Number Invited _____ Number Attending _____

❏Name: _____ Phone: _____ Gifts   Thank You
Children:_____ Shower: _____ ❏
Address:_____ Shower: _____ ❏
City: _____ State: _____ Zip: _____ Wedding:_____ ❏
Wedding Invitation: ❏ Reception Invitation: ❏ Announcements: ❏ RSVP: Yes ❏ No ❏ Number Invited _____ Number Attending _____

❑Name: _____ Phone: _____ Gifts   Thank You
Children:_____ Shower: _____ ❑
Address:_____ Shower: _____ ❑
City: _____ State: _____ Zip: _____ Wedding:_____ ❑
Wedding Invitation: ❑ Reception Invitation: ❑ Announcements: ❑ RSVP: Yes ❑ No ❑ Number Invited _____ Number Attending _____

❑Name: _____ Phone: _____ Gifts   Thank You
Children:_____ Shower: _____ ❑
Address:_____ Shower: _____ ❑
City: _____ State: _____ Zip: _____ Wedding:_____ ❑
Wedding Invitation: ❑ Reception Invitation: ❑ Announcements: ❑ RSVP: Yes ❑ No ❑ Number Invited _____ Number Attending _____

❑Name: _____ Phone: _____ Gifts   Thank You
Children:_____ Shower: _____ ❑
Address:_____ Shower: _____ ❑
City: _____ State: _____ Zip: _____ Wedding:_____ ❑
Wedding Invitation: ❑ Reception Invitation: ❑ Announcements: ❑ RSVP: Yes ❑ No ❑ Number Invited _____ Number Attending _____

❑Name: _____ Phone: _____ Gifts   Thank You
Children:_____ Shower: _____ ❑
Address:_____ Shower: _____ ❑
City: _____ State: _____ Zip: _____ Wedding:_____ ❑
Wedding Invitation: ❑ Reception Invitation: ❑ Announcements: ❑ RSVP: Yes ❑ No ❑ Number Invited _____ Number Attending _____

❑Name: _____ Phone: _____ Gifts   Thank You
Children:_____ Shower: _____ ❑
Address:_____ Shower: _____ ❑
City: _____ State: _____ Zip: _____ Wedding:_____ ❑
Wedding Invitation: ❑ Reception Invitation: ❑ Announcements: ❑ RSVP: Yes ❑ No ❑ Number Invited _____ Number Attending _____

❑Name: _____ Phone: _____ Gifts   Thank You
Children:_____ Shower: _____ ❑
Address:_____ Shower: _____ ❑
City: _____ State: _____ Zip: _____ Wedding:_____ ❑
Wedding Invitation: ❑ Reception Invitation: ❑ Announcements: ❑ RSVP: Yes ❑ No ❑ Number Invited _____ Number Attending _____

❑Name: _____ Phone: _____ Gifts   Thank You
Children:_____ Shower: _____ ❑
Address:_____ Shower: _____ ❑
City: _____ State: _____ Zip: _____ Wedding:_____ ❑
Wedding Invitation: ❑ Reception Invitation: ❑ Announcements: ❑ RSVP: Yes ❑ No ❑ Number Invited _____ Number Attending _____

Name: _____ Phone: _____ Gifts   Thank You
Children:_____ Shower: _____ ❑
Address:_____ Shower: _____ ❑
City: _____ State: _____ Zip: _____ Wedding:_____ ❑
Wedding Invitation: ❑ Reception Invitation: ❑ Announcements: ❑ RSVP: Yes ❑ No ❑ Number Invited _____ Number Attending _____

❑Name: _____ Phone: _____ Gifts   Thank You
Children:_____ Shower: _____ ❑
Address:_____ Shower: _____ ❑
City: _____ State: _____ Zip: _____ Wedding:_____ ❑
Wedding Invitation: ❑ Reception Invitation: ❑ Announcements: ❑ RSVP: Yes ❑ No ❑ Number Invited _____ Number Attending _____

❑Name: _____ Phone: _____ Gifts   Thank You
Children:_____ Shower: _____ ❑
Address:_____ Shower: _____ ❑
City: _____ State: _____ Zip: _____ Wedding:_____ ❑
Wedding Invitation: ❑ Reception Invitation: ❑ Announcements: ❑ RSVP: Yes ❑ No ❑ Number Invited _____ Number Attending _____

❑Name: _____ Phone: _____ Gifts   Thank You
Children:_____ Shower: _____ ❑
Address:_____ Shower: _____ ❑
City: _____ State: _____ Zip: _____ Wedding:_____ ❑
Wedding Invitation: ❑ Reception Invitation: ❑ Announcements: ❑ RSVP: Yes ❑ No ❑ Number Invited _____ Number Attending _____

❏Name: _____ Phone: _____ Gifts   Thank You
Children:_____ Shower: _____ ❏
Address:_____ Shower: _____ ❏
City: _____ State: _____ Zip: _____ Wedding:_____ ❏
Wedding Invitation: ❏ Reception Invitation: ❏ Announcements: ❏ RSVP: Yes ❏ No ❏ Number Invited _____ Number Attending _____

❏Name: _____ Phone: _____ Gifts   Thank You
Children:_____ Shower: _____ ❏
Address:_____ Shower: _____ ❏
City: _____ State: _____ Zip: _____ Wedding:_____ ❏
Wedding Invitation: ❏ Reception Invitation: ❏ Announcements: ❏ RSVP: Yes ❏ No ❏ Number Invited _____ Number Attending _____

❏Name: _____ Phone: _____ Gifts   Thank You
Children:_____ Shower: _____ ❏
Address:_____ Shower: _____ ❏
City: _____ State: _____ Zip: _____ Wedding:_____ ❏
Wedding Invitation: ❏ Reception Invitation: ❏ Announcements: ❏ RSVP: Yes ❏ No ❏ Number Invited _____ Number Attending _____

❏Name: _____ Phone: _____ Gifts   Thank You
Children:_____ Shower: _____ ❏
Address:_____ Shower: _____ ❏
City: _____ State: _____ Zip: _____ Wedding:_____ ❏
Wedding Invitation: ❏ Reception Invitation: ❏ Announcements: ❏ RSVP: Yes ❏ No ❏ Number Invited _____ Number Attending _____

❏Name: _____ Phone: _____ Gifts   Thank You
Children:_____ Shower: _____ ❏
Address:_____ Shower: _____ ❏
City: _____ State: _____ Zip: _____ Wedding:_____ ❏
Wedding Invitation: ❏ Reception Invitation: ❏ Announcements: ❏ RSVP: Yes ❏ No ❏ Number Invited _____ Number Attending _____

❏Name: _____ Phone: _____ Gifts   Thank You
Children:_____ Shower: _____ ❏
Address:_____ Shower: _____ ❏
City: _____ State: _____ Zip: _____ Wedding:_____ ❏
Wedding Invitation: ❏ Reception Invitation: ❏ Announcements: ❏ RSVP: Yes ❏ No ❏ Number Invited _____ Number Attending _____

❏Name: _____ Phone: _____ Gifts   Thank You
Children:_____ Shower: _____ ❏
Address:_____ Shower: _____ ❏
City: _____ State: _____ Zip: _____ Wedding:_____ ❏
Wedding Invitation: ❏ Reception Invitation: ❏ Announcements: ❏ RSVP: Yes ❏ No ❏ Number Invited _____ Number Attending _____

Name: _____ Phone: _____ Gifts   Thank You
Children:_____ Shower: _____ ❏
Address:_____ Shower: _____ ❏
City: _____ State: _____ Zip: _____ Wedding:_____ ❏
Wedding Invitation: ❏ Reception Invitation: ❏ Announcements: ❏ RSVP: Yes ❏ No ❏ Number Invited _____ Number Attending _____

❏Name: _____ Phone: _____ Gifts   Thank You
Children:_____ Shower: _____ ❏
Address:_____ Shower: _____ ❏
City: _____ State: _____ Zip: _____ Wedding:_____ ❏
Wedding Invitation: ❏ Reception Invitation: ❏ Announcements: ❏ RSVP: Yes ❏ No ❏ Number Invited _____ Number Attending _____

❏Name: _____ Phone: _____ Gifts   Thank You
Children:_____ Shower: _____ ❏
Address:_____ Shower: _____ ❏
City: _____ State: _____ Zip: _____ Wedding:_____ ❏
Wedding Invitation: ❏ Reception Invitation: ❏ Announcements: ❏ RSVP: Yes ❏ No ❏ Number Invited _____ Number Attending _____

❏Name: _____ Phone: _____ Gifts   Thank You
Children:_____ Shower: _____ ❏
Address:_____ Shower: _____ ❏
City: _____ State: _____ Zip: _____ Wedding:_____ ❏
Wedding Invitation: ❏ Reception Invitation: ❏ Announcements: ❏ RSVP: Yes ❏ No ❏ Number Invited _____ Number Attending _____

☐ Name: _____ Phone: _____ Gifts   Thank You
Children: _____ Shower: _____ ☐
Address: _____ Shower: _____ ☐
City: _____ State: _____ Zip: _____ Wedding: _____ ☐
Wedding Invitation: ☐ Reception Invitation: ☐ Announcements: ☐ RSVP: Yes ☐ No ☐ Number Invited _____ Number Attending _____

☐ Name: _____ Phone: _____ Gifts   Thank You
Children: _____ Shower: _____ ☐
Address: _____ Shower: _____ ☐
City: _____ State: _____ Zip: _____ Wedding: _____ ☐
Wedding Invitation: ☐ Reception Invitation: ☐ Announcements: ☐ RSVP: Yes ☐ No ☐ Number Invited _____ Number Attending _____

☐ Name: _____ Phone: _____ Gifts   Thank You
Children: _____ Shower: _____ ☐
Address: _____ Shower: _____ ☐
City: _____ State: _____ Zip: _____ Wedding: _____ ☐
Wedding Invitation: ☐ Reception Invitation: ☐ Announcements: ☐ RSVP: Yes ☐ No ☐ Number Invited _____ Number Attending _____

☐ Name: _____ Phone: _____ Gifts   Thank You
Children: _____ Shower: _____ ☐
Address: _____ Shower: _____ ☐
City: _____ State: _____ Zip: _____ Wedding: _____ ☐
Wedding Invitation: ☐ Reception Invitation: ☐ Announcements: ☐ RSVP: Yes ☐ No ☐ Number Invited _____ Number Attending _____

☐ Name: _____ Phone: _____ Gifts   Thank You
Children: _____ Shower: _____ ☐
Address: _____ Shower: _____ ☐
City: _____ State: _____ Zip: _____ Wedding: _____ ☐
Wedding Invitation: ☐ Reception Invitation: ☐ Announcements: ☐ RSVP: Yes ☐ No ☐ Number Invited _____ Number Attending _____

☐ Name: _____ Phone: _____ Gifts   Thank You
Children: _____ Shower: _____ ☐
Address: _____ Shower: _____ ☐
City: _____ State: _____ Zip: _____ Wedding: _____ ☐
Wedding Invitation: ☐ Reception Invitation: ☐ Announcements: ☐ RSVP: Yes ☐ No ☐ Number Invited _____ Number Attending _____

☐ Name: _____ Phone: _____ Gifts   Thank You
Children: _____ Shower: _____ ☐
Address: _____ Shower: _____ ☐
City: _____ State: _____ Zip: _____ Wedding: _____ ☐
Wedding Invitation: ☐ Reception Invitation: ☐ Announcements: ☐ RSVP: Yes ☐ No ☐ Number Invited _____ Number Attending _____

Name: _____ Phone: _____ Gifts   Thank You
Children: _____ Shower: _____ ☐
Address: _____ Shower: _____ ☐
City: _____ State: _____ Zip: _____ Wedding: _____ ☐
Wedding Invitation: ☐ Reception Invitation: ☐ Announcements: ☐ RSVP: Yes ☐ No ☐ Number Invited _____ Number Attending _____

☐ Name: _____ Phone: _____ Gifts   Thank You
Children: _____ Shower: _____ ☐
Address: _____ Shower: _____ ☐
City: _____ State: _____ Zip: _____ Wedding: _____ ☐
Wedding Invitation: ☐ Reception Invitation: ☐ Announcements: ☐ RSVP: Yes ☐ No ☐ Number Invited _____ Number Attending _____

☐ Name: _____ Phone: _____ Gifts   Thank You
Children: _____ Shower: _____ ☐
Address: _____ Shower: _____ ☐
City: _____ State: _____ Zip: _____ Wedding: _____ ☐
Wedding Invitation: ☐ Reception Invitation: ☐ Announcements: ☐ RSVP: Yes ☐ No ☐ Number Invited _____ Number Attending _____

☐ Name: _____ Phone: _____ Gifts   Thank You
Children: _____ Shower: _____ ☐
Address: _____ Shower: _____ ☐
City: _____ State: _____ Zip: _____ Wedding: _____ ☐
Wedding Invitation: ☐ Reception Invitation: ☐ Announcements: ☐ RSVP: Yes ☐ No ☐ Number Invited _____ Number Attending _____

❏Name: _____ Phone: _____ Gifts   Thank You
Children:_____ Shower: _____ ❏
Address:_____ Shower: _____ ❏
City: _____ State: _____ Zip: _____ Wedding:_____ ❏
Wedding Invitation: ❏ Reception Invitation: ❏ Announcements: ❏ RSVP: Yes ❏ No ❏ Number Invited _____ Number Attending _____

❏Name: _____ Phone: _____ Gifts   Thank You
Children:_____ Shower: _____ ❏
Address:_____ Shower: _____ ❏
City: _____ State: _____ Zip: _____ Wedding:_____ ❏
Wedding Invitation: ❏ Reception Invitation: ❏ Announcements: ❏ RSVP: Yes ❏ No ❏ Number Invited _____ Number Attending _____

❏Name: _____ Phone: _____ Gifts   Thank You
Children:_____ Shower: _____ ❏
Address:_____ Shower: _____ ❏
City: _____ State: _____ Zip: _____ Wedding:_____ ❏
Wedding Invitation: ❏ Reception Invitation: ❏ Announcements: ❏ RSVP: Yes ❏ No ❏ Number Invited _____ Number Attending _____

❏Name: _____ Phone: _____ Gifts   Thank You
Children:_____ Shower: _____ ❏
Address:_____ Shower: _____ ❏
City: _____ State: _____ Zip: _____ Wedding:_____ ❏
Wedding Invitation: ❏ Reception Invitation: ❏ Announcements: ❏ RSVP: Yes ❏ No ❏ Number Invited _____ Number Attending _____

❏Name: _____ Phone: _____ Gifts   Thank You
Children:_____ Shower: _____ ❏
Address:_____ Shower: _____ ❏
City: _____ State: _____ Zip: _____ Wedding:_____ ❏
Wedding Invitation: ❏ Reception Invitation: ❏ Announcements: ❏ RSVP: Yes ❏ No ❏ Number Invited _____ Number Attending _____

❏Name: _____ Phone: _____ Gifts   Thank You
Children:_____ Shower: _____ ❏
Address:_____ Shower: _____ ❏
City: _____ State: _____ Zip: _____ Wedding:_____ ❏
Wedding Invitation: ❏ Reception Invitation: ❏ Announcements: ❏ RSVP: Yes ❏ No ❏ Number Invited _____ Number Attending _____

❏Name: _____ Phone: _____ Gifts   Thank You
Children:_____ Shower: _____ ❏
Address:_____ Shower: _____ ❏
City: _____ State: _____ Zip: _____ Wedding:_____ ❏
Wedding Invitation: ❏ Reception Invitation: ❏ Announcements: ❏ RSVP: Yes ❏ No ❏ Number Invited _____ Number Attending _____

Name: _____ Phone: _____ Gifts   Thank You
Children:_____ Shower: _____ ❏
Address:_____ Shower: _____ ❏
City: _____ State: _____ Zip: _____ Wedding:_____ ❏
Wedding Invitation: ❏ Reception Invitation: ❏ Announcements: ❏ RSVP: Yes ❏ No ❏ Number Invited _____ Number Attending _____

❏Name: _____ Phone: _____ Gifts   Thank You
Children:_____ Shower: _____ ❏
Address:_____ Shower: _____ ❏
City: _____ State: _____ Zip: _____ Wedding:_____ ❏
Wedding Invitation: ❏ Reception Invitation: ❏ Announcements: ❏ RSVP: Yes ❏ No ❏ Number Invited _____ Number Attending _____

❏Name: _____ Phone: _____ Gifts   Thank You
Children:_____ Shower: _____ ❏
Address:_____ Shower: _____ ❏
City: _____ State: _____ Zip: _____ Wedding:_____ ❏
Wedding Invitation: ❏ Reception Invitation: ❏ Announcements: ❏ RSVP: Yes ❏ No ❏ Number Invited _____ Number Attending _____

❏Name: _____ Phone: _____ Gifts   Thank You
Children:_____ Shower: _____ ❏
Address:_____ Shower: _____ ❏
City: _____ State: _____ Zip: _____ Wedding:_____ ❏
Wedding Invitation: ❏ Reception Invitation: ❏ Announcements: ❏ RSVP: Yes ❏ No ❏ Number Invited _____ Number Attending _____

❑Name: _____ Phone: _____ Gifts   Thank You
Children:_____ Shower: _____ ❑
Address:_____ Shower: _____ ❑
City: _____ State: _____ Zip: _____ Wedding: _____ ❑
Wedding Invitation: ❑ Reception Invitation: ❑ Announcements: ❑ RSVP: Yes ❑ No ❑ Number Invited _____ Number Attending _____

❑Name: _____ Phone: _____ Gifts   Thank You
Children:_____ Shower: _____ ❑
Address:_____ Shower: _____ ❑
City: _____ State: _____ Zip: _____ Wedding: _____ ❑
Wedding Invitation: ❑ Reception Invitation: ❑ Announcements: ❑ RSVP: Yes ❑ No ❑ Number Invited _____ Number Attending _____

❑Name: _____ Phone: _____ Gifts   Thank You
Children:_____ Shower: _____ ❑
Address:_____ Shower: _____ ❑
City: _____ State: _____ Zip: _____ Wedding: _____ ❑
Wedding Invitation: ❑ Reception Invitation: ❑ Announcements: ❑ RSVP: Yes ❑ No ❑ Number Invited _____ Number Attending _____

❑Name: _____ Phone: _____ Gifts   Thank You
Children:_____ Shower: _____ ❑
Address:_____ Shower: _____ ❑
City: _____ State: _____ Zip: _____ Wedding: _____ ❑
Wedding Invitation: ❑ Reception Invitation: ❑ Announcements: ❑ RSVP: Yes ❑ No ❑ Number Invited _____ Number Attending _____

❑Name: _____ Phone: _____ Gifts   Thank You
Children:_____ Shower: _____ ❑
Address:_____ Shower: _____ ❑
City: _____ State: _____ Zip: _____ Wedding: _____ ❑
Wedding Invitation: ❑ Reception Invitation: ❑ Announcements: ❑ RSVP: Yes ❑ No ❑ Number Invited _____ Number Attending _____

❑Name: _____ Phone: _____ Gifts   Thank You
Children:_____ Shower: _____ ❑
Address:_____ Shower: _____ ❑
City: _____ State: _____ Zip: _____ Wedding: _____ ❑
Wedding Invitation: ❑ Reception Invitation: ❑ Announcements: ❑ RSVP: Yes ❑ No ❑ Number Invited _____ Number Attending _____

❑Name: _____ Phone: _____ Gifts   Thank You
Children:_____ Shower: _____ ❑
Address:_____ Shower: _____ ❑
City: _____ State: _____ Zip: _____ Wedding: _____ ❑
Wedding Invitation: ❑ Reception Invitation: ❑ Announcements: ❑ RSVP: Yes ❑ No ❑ Number Invited _____ Number Attending _____

Name: _____ Phone: _____ Gifts   Thank You
Children:_____ Shower: _____ ❑
Address:_____ Shower: _____ ❑
City: _____ State: _____ Zip: _____ Wedding: _____ ❑
Wedding Invitation: ❑ Reception Invitation: ❑ Announcements: ❑ RSVP: Yes ❑ No ❑ Number Invited _____ Number Attending _____

❑Name: _____ Phone: _____ Gifts   Thank You
Children:_____ Shower: _____ ❑
Address:_____ Shower: _____ ❑
City: _____ State: _____ Zip: _____ Wedding: _____ ❑
Wedding Invitation: ❑ Reception Invitation: ❑ Announcements: ❑ RSVP: Yes ❑ No ❑ Number Invited _____ Number Attending _____

❑Name: _____ Phone: _____ Gifts   Thank You
Children:_____ Shower: _____ ❑
Address:_____ Shower: _____ ❑
City: _____ State: _____ Zip: _____ Wedding: _____ ❑
Wedding Invitation: ❑ Reception Invitation: ❑ Announcements: ❑ RSVP: Yes ❑ No ❑ Number Invited _____ Number Attending _____

❑Name: _____ Phone: _____ Gifts   Thank You
Children:_____ Shower: _____ ❑
Address:_____ Shower: _____ ❑
City: _____ State: _____ Zip: _____ Wedding: _____ ❑
Wedding Invitation: ❑ Reception Invitation: ❑ Announcements: ❑ RSVP: Yes ❑ No ❑ Number Invited _____ Number Attending _____

❑Name: _____ Phone: _____ Gifts   Thank You
Children:_____ Shower: _____ ❑
Address:_____ Shower: _____ ❑
City: _____ State: _____ Zip: _____ Wedding:_____ ❑
Wedding Invitation: ❑ Reception Invitation: ❑ Announcements: ❑ RSVP: Yes ❑ No ❑ Number Invited _____ Number Attending _____

❑Name: _____ Phone: _____ Gifts   Thank You
Children:_____ Shower: _____ ❑
Address:_____ Shower: _____ ❑
City: _____ State: _____ Zip: _____ Wedding:_____ ❑
Wedding Invitation: ❑ Reception Invitation: ❑ Announcements: ❑ RSVP: Yes ❑ No ❑ Number Invited _____ Number Attending _____

❑Name: _____ Phone: _____ Gifts   Thank You
Children:_____ Shower: _____ ❑
Address:_____ Shower: _____ ❑
City: _____ State: _____ Zip: _____ Wedding:_____ ❑
Wedding Invitation: ❑ Reception Invitation: ❑ Announcements: ❑ RSVP: Yes ❑ No ❑ Number Invited _____ Number Attending _____

❑Name: _____ Phone: _____ Gifts   Thank You
Children:_____ Shower: _____ ❑
Address:_____ Shower: _____ ❑
City: _____ State: _____ Zip: _____ Wedding:_____ ❑
Wedding Invitation: ❑ Reception Invitation: ❑ Announcements: ❑ RSVP: Yes ❑ No ❑ Number Invited _____ Number Attending _____

❑Name: _____ Phone: _____ Gifts   Thank You
Children:_____ Shower: _____ ❑
Address:_____ Shower: _____ ❑
City: _____ State: _____ Zip: _____ Wedding:_____ ❑
Wedding Invitation: ❑ Reception Invitation: ❑ Announcements: ❑ RSVP: Yes ❑ No ❑ Number Invited _____ Number Attending _____

❑Name: _____ Phone: _____ Gifts   Thank You
Children:_____ Shower: _____ ❑
Address:_____ Shower: _____ ❑
City: _____ State: _____ Zip: _____ Wedding:_____ ❑
Wedding Invitation: ❑ Reception Invitation: ❑ Announcements: ❑ RSVP: Yes ❑ No ❑ Number Invited _____ Number Attending _____

❑Name: _____ Phone: _____ Gifts   Thank You
Children:_____ Shower: _____ ❑
Address:_____ Shower: _____ ❑
City: _____ State: _____ Zip: _____ Wedding:_____ ❑
Wedding Invitation: ❑ Reception Invitation: ❑ Announcements: ❑ RSVP: Yes ❑ No ❑ Number Invited _____ Number Attending _____

Name: _____ Phone: _____ Gifts   Thank You
Children:_____ Shower: _____ ❑
Address:_____ Shower: _____ ❑
City: _____ State: _____ Zip: _____ Wedding:_____ ❑
Wedding Invitation: ❑ Reception Invitation: ❑ Announcements: ❑ RSVP: Yes ❑ No ❑ Number Invited _____ Number Attending _____

❑Name: _____ Phone: _____ Gifts   Thank You
Children:_____ Shower: _____ ❑
Address:_____ Shower: _____ ❑
City: _____ State: _____ Zip: _____ Wedding:_____ ❑
Wedding Invitation: ❑ Reception Invitation: ❑ Announcements: ❑ RSVP: Yes ❑ No ❑ Number Invited _____ Number Attending _____

❑Name: _____ Phone: _____ Gifts   Thank You
Children:_____ Shower: _____ ❑
Address:_____ Shower: _____ ❑
City: _____ State: _____ Zip: _____ Wedding:_____ ❑
Wedding Invitation: ❑ Reception Invitation: ❑ Announcements: ❑ RSVP: Yes ❑ No ❑ Number Invited _____ Number Attending _____

❑Name: _____ Phone: _____ Gifts   Thank You
Children:_____ Shower: _____ ❑
Address:_____ Shower: _____ ❑
City: _____ State: _____ Zip: _____ Wedding:_____ ❑
Wedding Invitation: ❑ Reception Invitation: ❑ Announcements: ❑ RSVP: Yes ❑ No ❑ Number Invited _____ Number Attending _____

❑Name: _____ Phone: _____ Gifts
Children: _____ Shower: _____ ❑ Thank You
Address: _____ Shower: _____ ❑
City: _____ State: _____ Zip: _____ Wedding: _____ ❑
Wedding Invitation: ❑ Reception Invitation: ❑ Announcements: ❑ RSVP: Yes ❑ No ❑ Number Invited _____ Number Attending _____

❑Name: _____ Phone: _____ Gifts
Children: _____ Shower: _____ ❑ Thank You
Address: _____ Shower: _____ ❑
City: _____ State: _____ Zip: _____ Wedding: _____ ❑
Wedding Invitation: ❑ Reception Invitation: ❑ Announcements: ❑ RSVP: Yes ❑ No ❑ Number Invited _____ Number Attending _____

❑Name: _____ Phone: _____ Gifts
Children: _____ Shower: _____ ❑ Thank You
Address: _____ Shower: _____ ❑
City: _____ State: _____ Zip: _____ Wedding: _____ ❑
Wedding Invitation: ❑ Reception Invitation: ❑ Announcements: ❑ RSVP: Yes ❑ No ❑ Number Invited _____ Number Attending _____

❑Name: _____ Phone: _____ Gifts
Children: _____ Shower: _____ ❑ Thank You
Address: _____ Shower: _____ ❑
City: _____ State: _____ Zip: _____ Wedding: _____ ❑
Wedding Invitation: ❑ Reception Invitation: ❑ Announcements: ❑ RSVP: Yes ❑ No ❑ Number Invited _____ Number Attending _____

❑Name: _____ Phone: _____ Gifts
Children: _____ Shower: _____ ❑ Thank You
Address: _____ Shower: _____ ❑
City: _____ State: _____ Zip: _____ Wedding: _____ ❑
Wedding Invitation: ❑ Reception Invitation: ❑ Announcements: ❑ RSVP: Yes ❑ No ❑ Number Invited _____ Number Attending _____

❑Name: _____ Phone: _____ Gifts
Children: _____ Shower: _____ ❑ Thank You
Address: _____ Shower: _____ ❑
City: _____ State: _____ Zip: _____ Wedding: _____ ❑
Wedding Invitation: ❑ Reception Invitation: ❑ Announcements: ❑ RSVP: Yes ❑ No ❑ Number Invited _____ Number Attending _____

❑Name: _____ Phone: _____ Gifts
Children: _____ Shower: _____ ❑ Thank You
Address: _____ Shower: _____ ❑
City: _____ State: _____ Zip: _____ Wedding: _____ ❑
Wedding Invitation: ❑ Reception Invitation: ❑ Announcements: ❑ RSVP: Yes ❑ No ❑ Number Invited _____ Number Attending _____

Name: _____ Phone: _____ Gifts
Children: _____ Shower: _____ ❑ Thank You
Address: _____ Shower: _____ ❑
City: _____ State: _____ Zip: _____ Wedding: _____ ❑
Wedding Invitation: ❑ Reception Invitation: ❑ Announcements: ❑ RSVP: Yes ❑ No ❑ Number Invited _____ Number Attending _____

❑Name: _____ Phone: _____ Gifts
Children: _____ Shower: _____ ❑ Thank You
Address: _____ Shower: _____ ❑
City: _____ State: _____ Zip: _____ Wedding: _____ ❑
Wedding Invitation: ❑ Reception Invitation: ❑ Announcements: ❑ RSVP: Yes ❑ No ❑ Number Invited _____ Number Attending _____

❑Name: _____ Phone: _____ Gifts
Children: _____ Shower: _____ ❑ Thank You
Address: _____ Shower: _____ ❑
City: _____ State: _____ Zip: _____ Wedding: _____ ❑
Wedding Invitation: ❑ Reception Invitation: ❑ Announcements: ❑ RSVP: Yes ❑ No ❑ Number Invited _____ Number Attending _____

❑Name: _____ Phone: _____ Gifts
Children: _____ Shower: _____ ❑ Thank You
Address: _____ Shower: _____ ❑
City: _____ State: _____ Zip: _____ Wedding: _____ ❑
Wedding Invitation: ❑ Reception Invitation: ❑ Announcements: ❑ RSVP: Yes ❑ No ❑ Number Invited _____ Number Attending _____

❑Name: _____ Phone: _____ Gifts   Thank You
Children:_____ Shower: _____ ❑
Address:_____ Shower: _____ ❑
City: _____ State: _____ Zip: _____ Wedding:_____ ❑
Wedding Invitation: ❑ Reception Invitation: ❑ Announcements: ❑ RSVP: Yes ❑ No ❑ Number Invited _____ Number Attending _____

❑Name: _____ Phone: _____ Gifts   Thank You
Children:_____ Shower: _____ ❑
Address:_____ Shower: _____ ❑
City: _____ State: _____ Zip: _____ Wedding:_____ ❑
Wedding Invitation: ❑ Reception Invitation: ❑ Announcements: ❑ RSVP: Yes ❑ No ❑ Number Invited _____ Number Attending _____

❑Name: _____ Phone: _____ Gifts   Thank You
Children:_____ Shower: _____ ❑
Address:_____ Shower: _____ ❑
City: _____ State: _____ Zip: _____ Wedding:_____ ❑
Wedding Invitation: ❑ Reception Invitation: ❑ Announcements: ❑ RSVP: Yes ❑ No ❑ Number Invited _____ Number Attending _____

❑Name: _____ Phone: _____ Gifts   Thank You
Children:_____ Shower: _____ ❑
Address:_____ Shower: _____ ❑
City: _____ State: _____ Zip: _____ Wedding:_____ ❑
Wedding Invitation: ❑ Reception Invitation: ❑ Announcements: ❑ RSVP: Yes ❑ No ❑ Number Invited _____ Number Attending _____

❑Name: _____ Phone: _____ Gifts   Thank You
Children:_____ Shower: _____ ❑
Address:_____ Shower: _____ ❑
City: _____ State: _____ Zip: _____ Wedding:_____ ❑
Wedding Invitation: ❑ Reception Invitation: ❑ Announcements: ❑ RSVP: Yes ❑ No ❑ Number Invited _____ Number Attending _____

❑Name: _____ Phone: _____ Gifts   Thank You
Children:_____ Shower: _____ ❑
Address:_____ Shower: _____ ❑
City: _____ State: _____ Zip: _____ Wedding:_____ ❑
Wedding Invitation: ❑ Reception Invitation: ❑ Announcements: ❑ RSVP: Yes ❑ No ❑ Number Invited _____ Number Attending _____

❑Name: _____ Phone: _____ Gifts   Thank You
Children:_____ Shower: _____ ❑
Address:_____ Shower: _____ ❑
City: _____ State: _____ Zip: _____ Wedding:_____ ❑
Wedding Invitation: ❑ Reception Invitation: ❑ Announcements: ❑ RSVP: Yes ❑ No ❑ Number Invited _____ Number Attending _____

Name: _____ Phone: _____ Gifts   Thank You
Children:_____ Shower: _____ ❑
Address:_____ Shower: _____ ❑
City: _____ State: _____ Zip: _____ Wedding:_____ ❑
Wedding Invitation: ❑ Reception Invitation: ❑ Announcements: ❑ RSVP: Yes ❑ No ❑ Number Invited _____ Number Attending _____

❑Name: _____ Phone: _____ Gifts   Thank You
Children:_____ Shower: _____ ❑
Address:_____ Shower: _____ ❑
City: _____ State: _____ Zip: _____ Wedding:_____ ❑
Wedding Invitation: ❑ Reception Invitation: ❑ Announcements: ❑ RSVP: Yes ❑ No ❑ Number Invited _____ Number Attending _____

❑Name: _____ Phone: _____ Gifts   Thank You
Children:_____ Shower: _____ ❑
Address:_____ Shower: _____ ❑
City: _____ State: _____ Zip: _____ Wedding:_____ ❑
Wedding Invitation: ❑ Reception Invitation: ❑ Announcements: ❑ RSVP: Yes ❑ No ❑ Number Invited _____ Number Attending _____

❑Name: _____ Phone: _____ Gifts   Thank You
Children:_____ Shower: _____ ❑
Address:_____ Shower: _____ ❑
City: _____ State: _____ Zip: _____ Wedding:_____ ❑
Wedding Invitation: ❑ Reception Invitation: ❑ Announcements: ❑ RSVP: Yes ❑ No ❑ Number Invited _____ Number Attending _____

❑Name: _____ Phone: _____ Gifts _____ Thank You
Children: _____ Shower: _____ ❑
Address: _____ Shower: _____ ❑
City: _____ State: _____ Zip: _____ Wedding: _____ ❑
Wedding Invitation: ❑ Reception Invitation: ❑ Announcements: ❑ RSVP: Yes ❑ No ❑ Number Invited _____ Number Attending _____

❑Name: _____ Phone: _____ Gifts _____ Thank You
Children: _____ Shower: _____ ❑
Address: _____ Shower: _____ ❑
City: _____ State: _____ Zip: _____ Wedding: _____ ❑
Wedding Invitation: ❑ Reception Invitation: ❑ Announcements: ❑ RSVP: Yes ❑ No ❑ Number Invited _____ Number Attending _____

❑Name: _____ Phone: _____ Gifts _____ Thank You
Children: _____ Shower: _____ ❑
Address: _____ Shower: _____ ❑
City: _____ State: _____ Zip: _____ Wedding: _____ ❑
Wedding Invitation: ❑ Reception Invitation: ❑ Announcements: ❑ RSVP: Yes ❑ No ❑ Number Invited _____ Number Attending _____

❑Name: _____ Phone: _____ Gifts _____ Thank You
Children: _____ Shower: _____ ❑
Address: _____ Shower: _____ ❑
City: _____ State: _____ Zip: _____ Wedding: _____ ❑
Wedding Invitation: ❑ Reception Invitation: ❑ Announcements: ❑ RSVP: Yes ❑ No ❑ Number Invited _____ Number Attending _____

❑Name: _____ Phone: _____ Gifts _____ Thank You
Children: _____ Shower: _____ ❑
Address: _____ Shower: _____ ❑
City: _____ State: _____ Zip: _____ Wedding: _____ ❑
Wedding Invitation: ❑ Reception Invitation: ❑ Announcements: ❑ RSVP: Yes ❑ No ❑ Number Invited _____ Number Attending _____

❑Name: _____ Phone: _____ Gifts _____ Thank You
Children: _____ Shower: _____ ❑
Address: _____ Shower: _____ ❑
City: _____ State: _____ Zip: _____ Wedding: _____ ❑
Wedding Invitation: ❑ Reception Invitation: ❑ Announcements: ❑ RSVP: Yes ❑ No ❑ Number Invited _____ Number Attending _____

❑Name: _____ Phone: _____ Gifts _____ Thank You
Children: _____ Shower: _____ ❑
Address: _____ Shower: _____ ❑
City: _____ State: _____ Zip: _____ Wedding: _____ ❑
Wedding Invitation: ❑ Reception Invitation: ❑ Announcements: ❑ RSVP: Yes ❑ No ❑ Number Invited _____ Number Attending _____

Name: _____ Phone: _____ Gifts _____ Thank You
Children: _____ Shower: _____ ❑
Address: _____ Shower: _____ ❑
City: _____ State: _____ Zip: _____ Wedding: _____ ❑
Wedding Invitation: ❑ Reception Invitation: ❑ Announcements: ❑ RSVP: Yes ❑ No ❑ Number Invited _____ Number Attending _____

❑Name: _____ Phone: _____ Gifts _____ Thank You
Children: _____ Shower: _____ ❑
Address: _____ Shower: _____ ❑
City: _____ State: _____ Zip: _____ Wedding: _____ ❑
Wedding Invitation: ❑ Reception Invitation: ❑ Announcements: ❑ RSVP: Yes ❑ No ❑ Number Invited _____ Number Attending _____

❑Name: _____ Phone: _____ Gifts _____ Thank You
Children: _____ Shower: _____ ❑
Address: _____ Shower: _____ ❑
City: _____ State: _____ Zip: _____ Wedding: _____ ❑
Wedding Invitation: ❑ Reception Invitation: ❑ Announcements: ❑ RSVP: Yes ❑ No ❑ Number Invited _____ Number Attending _____

❑Name: _____ Phone: _____ Gifts _____ Thank You
Children: _____ Shower: _____ ❑
Address: _____ Shower: _____ ❑
City: _____ State: _____ Zip: _____ Wedding: _____ ❑
Wedding Invitation: ❑ Reception Invitation: ❑ Announcements: ❑ RSVP: Yes ❑ No ❑ Number Invited _____ Number Attending _____

❑Name: _____ Phone: _____ Gifts ⠀⠀⠀⠀Thank You
Children:_____ Shower: _____ ❑
Address:_____ Shower: _____ ❑
City: _____ State: _____ Zip: _____ Wedding:_____ ❑
Wedding Invitation: ❑ Reception Invitation: ❑ Announcements: ❑ RSVP: Yes ❑ No ❑ Number Invited _____ Number Attending _____

❑Name: _____ Phone: _____ Gifts ⠀⠀⠀⠀Thank You
Children:_____ Shower: _____ ❑
Address:_____ Shower: _____ ❑
City: _____ State: _____ Zip: _____ Wedding:_____ ❑
Wedding Invitation: ❑ Reception Invitation: ❑ Announcements: ❑ RSVP: Yes ❑ No ❑ Number Invited _____ Number Attending _____

❑Name: _____ Phone: _____ Gifts ⠀⠀⠀⠀Thank You
Children:_____ Shower: _____ ❑
Address:_____ Shower: _____ ❑
City: _____ State: _____ Zip: _____ Wedding:_____ ❑
Wedding Invitation: ❑ Reception Invitation: ❑ Announcements: ❑ RSVP: Yes ❑ No ❑ Number Invited _____ Number Attending _____

❑Name: _____ Phone: _____ Gifts ⠀⠀⠀⠀Thank You
Children:_____ Shower: _____ ❑
Address:_____ Shower: _____ ❑
City: _____ State: _____ Zip: _____ Wedding:_____ ❑
Wedding Invitation: ❑ Reception Invitation: ❑ Announcements: ❑ RSVP: Yes ❑ No ❑ Number Invited _____ Number Attending _____

❑Name: _____ Phone: _____ Gifts ⠀⠀⠀⠀Thank You
Children:_____ Shower: _____ ❑
Address:_____ Shower: _____ ❑
City: _____ State: _____ Zip: _____ Wedding:_____ ❑
Wedding Invitation: ❑ Reception Invitation: ❑ Announcements: ❑ RSVP: Yes ❑ No ❑ Number Invited _____ Number Attending _____

❑Name: _____ Phone: _____ Gifts ⠀⠀⠀⠀Thank You
Children:_____ Shower: _____ ❑
Address:_____ Shower: _____ ❑
City: _____ State: _____ Zip: _____ Wedding:_____ ❑
Wedding Invitation: ❑ Reception Invitation: ❑ Announcements: ❑ RSVP: Yes ❑ No ❑ Number Invited _____ Number Attending _____

❑Name: _____ Phone: _____ Gifts ⠀⠀⠀⠀Thank You
Children:_____ Shower: _____ ❑
Address:_____ Shower: _____ ❑
City: _____ State: _____ Zip: _____ Wedding:_____ ❑
Wedding Invitation: ❑ Reception Invitation: ❑ Announcements: ❑ RSVP: Yes ❑ No ❑ Number Invited _____ Number Attending _____

Name: _____ Phone: _____ Gifts ⠀⠀⠀⠀Thank You
Children:_____ Shower: _____ ❑
Address:_____ Shower: _____ ❑
City: _____ State: _____ Zip: _____ Wedding:_____ ❑
Wedding Invitation: ❑ Reception Invitation: ❑ Announcements: ❑ RSVP: Yes ❑ No ❑ Number Invited _____ Number Attending _____

❑Name: _____ Phone: _____ Gifts ⠀⠀⠀⠀Thank You
Children:_____ Shower: _____ ❑
Address:_____ Shower: _____ ❑
City: _____ State: _____ Zip: _____ Wedding:_____ ❑
Wedding Invitation: ❑ Reception Invitation: ❑ Announcements: ❑ RSVP: Yes ❑ No ❑ Number Invited _____ Number Attending _____

❑Name: _____ Phone: _____ Gifts ⠀⠀⠀⠀Thank You
Children:_____ Shower: _____ ❑
Address:_____ Shower: _____ ❑
City: _____ State: _____ Zip: _____ Wedding:_____ ❑
Wedding Invitation: ❑ Reception Invitation: ❑ Announcements: ❑ RSVP: Yes ❑ No ❑ Number Invited _____ Number Attending _____

❑Name: _____ Phone: _____ Gifts ⠀⠀⠀⠀Thank You
Children:_____ Shower: _____ ❑
Address:_____ Shower: _____ ❑
City: _____ State: _____ Zip: _____ Wedding:_____ ❑
Wedding Invitation: ❑ Reception Invitation: ❑ Announcements: ❑ RSVP: Yes ❑ No ❑ Number Invited _____ Number Attending _____

❑Name: _____ Phone: _____ Gifts   Thank You
Children:_____ Shower: _____ ❑
Address:_____ Shower: _____ ❑
City: _____ State: _____ Zip: _____ Wedding:_____ ❑
Wedding Invitation: ❑ Reception Invitation: ❑ Announcements: ❑ RSVP: Yes ❑ No ❑ Number Invited _____ Number Attending _____

❑Name: _____ Phone: _____ Gifts   Thank You
Children:_____ Shower: _____ ❑
Address:_____ Shower: _____ ❑
City: _____ State: _____ Zip: _____ Wedding:_____ ❑
Wedding Invitation: ❑ Reception Invitation: ❑ Announcements: ❑ RSVP: Yes ❑ No ❑ Number Invited _____ Number Attending _____

❑Name: _____ Phone: _____ Gifts   Thank You
Children:_____ Shower: _____ ❑
Address:_____ Shower: _____ ❑
City: _____ State: _____ Zip: _____ Wedding:_____ ❑
Wedding Invitation: ❑ Reception Invitation: ❑ Announcements: ❑ RSVP: Yes ❑ No ❑ Number Invited _____ Number Attending _____

❑Name: _____ Phone: _____ Gifts   Thank You
Children:_____ Shower: _____ ❑
Address:_____ Shower: _____ ❑
City: _____ State: _____ Zip: _____ Wedding:_____ ❑
Wedding Invitation: ❑ Reception Invitation: ❑ Announcements: ❑ RSVP: Yes ❑ No ❑ Number Invited _____ Number Attending _____

❑Name: _____ Phone: _____ Gifts   Thank You
Children:_____ Shower: _____ ❑
Address:_____ Shower: _____ ❑
City: _____ State: _____ Zip: _____ Wedding:_____ ❑
Wedding Invitation: ❑ Reception Invitation: ❑ Announcements: ❑ RSVP: Yes ❑ No ❑ Number Invited _____ Number Attending _____

❑Name: _____ Phone: _____ Gifts   Thank You
Children:_____ Shower: _____ ❑
Address:_____ Shower: _____ ❑
City: _____ State: _____ Zip: _____ Wedding:_____ ❑
Wedding Invitation: ❑ Reception Invitation: ❑ Announcements: ❑ RSVP: Yes ❑ No ❑ Number Invited _____ Number Attending _____

❑Name: _____ Phone: _____ Gifts   Thank You
Children:_____ Shower: _____ ❑
Address:_____ Shower: _____ ❑
City: _____ State: _____ Zip: _____ Wedding:_____ ❑
Wedding Invitation: ❑ Reception Invitation: ❑ Announcements: ❑ RSVP: Yes ❑ No ❑ Number Invited _____ Number Attending _____

Name: _____ Phone: _____ Gifts   Thank You
Children:_____ Shower: _____ ❑
Address:_____ Shower: _____ ❑
City: _____ State: _____ Zip: _____ Wedding:_____ ❑
Wedding Invitation: ❑ Reception Invitation: ❑ Announcements: ❑ RSVP: Yes ❑ No ❑ Number Invited _____ Number Attending _____

❑Name: _____ Phone: _____ Gifts   Thank You
Children:_____ Shower: _____ ❑
Address:_____ Shower: _____ ❑
City: _____ State: _____ Zip: _____ Wedding:_____ ❑
Wedding Invitation: ❑ Reception Invitation: ❑ Announcements: ❑ RSVP: Yes ❑ No ❑ Number Invited _____ Number Attending _____

❑Name: _____ Phone: _____ Gifts   Thank You
Children:_____ Shower: _____ ❑
Address:_____ Shower: _____ ❑
City: _____ State: _____ Zip: _____ Wedding:_____ ❑
Wedding Invitation: ❑ Reception Invitation: ❑ Announcements: ❑ RSVP: Yes ❑ No ❑ Number Invited _____ Number Attending _____

❑Name: _____ Phone: _____ Gifts   Thank You
Children:_____ Shower: _____ ❑
Address:_____ Shower: _____ ❑
City: _____ State: _____ Zip: _____ Wedding:_____ ❑
Wedding Invitation: ❑ Reception Invitation: ❑ Announcements: ❑ RSVP: Yes ❑ No ❑ Number Invited _____ Number Attending _____

❏Name: _____ Phone: _____ Gifts   Thank You
Children: _____ Shower: _____ ❏
Address: _____ Shower: _____ ❏
City: _____ State: _____ Zip: _____ Wedding: _____ ❏
Wedding Invitation: ❏ Reception Invitation: ❏ Announcements: ❏ RSVP: Yes ❏ No ❏ Number Invited _____ Number Attending _____

❏Name: _____ Phone: _____ Gifts   Thank You
Children: _____ Shower: _____ ❏
Address: _____ Shower: _____ ❏
City: _____ State: _____ Zip: _____ Wedding: _____ ❏
Wedding Invitation: ❏ Reception Invitation: ❏ Announcements: ❏ RSVP: Yes ❏ No ❏ Number Invited _____ Number Attending _____

❏Name: _____ Phone: _____ Gifts   Thank You
Children: _____ Shower: _____ ❏
Address: _____ Shower: _____ ❏
City: _____ State: _____ Zip: _____ Wedding: _____ ❏
Wedding Invitation: ❏ Reception Invitation: ❏ Announcements: ❏ RSVP: Yes ❏ No ❏ Number Invited _____ Number Attending _____

❏Name: _____ Phone: _____ Gifts   Thank You
Children: _____ Shower: _____ ❏
Address: _____ Shower: _____ ❏
City: _____ State: _____ Zip: _____ Wedding: _____ ❏
Wedding Invitation: ❏ Reception Invitation: ❏ Announcements: ❏ RSVP: Yes ❏ No ❏ Number Invited _____ Number Attending _____

❏Name: _____ Phone: _____ Gifts   Thank You
Children: _____ Shower: _____ ❏
Address: _____ Shower: _____ ❏
City: _____ State: _____ Zip: _____ Wedding: _____ ❏
Wedding Invitation: ❏ Reception Invitation: ❏ Announcements: ❏ RSVP: Yes ❏ No ❏ Number Invited _____ Number Attending _____

❏Name: _____ Phone: _____ Gifts   Thank You
Children: _____ Shower: _____ ❏
Address: _____ Shower: _____ ❏
City: _____ State: _____ Zip: _____ Wedding: _____ ❏
Wedding Invitation: ❏ Reception Invitation: ❏ Announcements: ❏ RSVP: Yes ❏ No ❏ Number Invited _____ Number Attending _____

❏Name: _____ Phone: _____ Gifts   Thank You
Children: _____ Shower: _____ ❏
Address: _____ Shower: _____ ❏
City: _____ State: _____ Zip: _____ Wedding: _____ ❏
Wedding Invitation: ❏ Reception Invitation: ❏ Announcements: ❏ RSVP: Yes ❏ No ❏ Number Invited _____ Number Attending _____

Name: _____ Phone: _____ Gifts   Thank You
Children: _____ Shower: _____ ❏
Address: _____ Shower: _____ ❏
City: _____ State: _____ Zip: _____ Wedding: _____ ❏
Wedding Invitation: ❏ Reception Invitation: ❏ Announcements: ❏ RSVP: Yes ❏ No ❏ Number Invited _____ Number Attending _____

❏Name: _____ Phone: _____ Gifts   Thank You
Children: _____ Shower: _____ ❏
Address: _____ Shower: _____ ❏
City: _____ State: _____ Zip: _____ Wedding: _____ ❏
Wedding Invitation: ❏ Reception Invitation: ❏ Announcements: ❏ RSVP: Yes ❏ No ❏ Number Invited _____ Number Attending _____

❏Name: _____ Phone: _____ Gifts   Thank You
Children: _____ Shower: _____ ❏
Address: _____ Shower: _____ ❏
City: _____ State: _____ Zip: _____ Wedding: _____ ❏
Wedding Invitation: ❏ Reception Invitation: ❏ Announcements: ❏ RSVP: Yes ❏ No ❏ Number Invited _____ Number Attending _____

❏Name: _____ Phone: _____ Gifts   Thank You
Children: _____ Shower: _____ ❏
Address: _____ Shower: _____ ❏
City: _____ State: _____ Zip: _____ Wedding: _____ ❏
Wedding Invitation: ❏ Reception Invitation: ❏ Announcements: ❏ RSVP: Yes ❏ No ❏ Number Invited _____ Number Attending _____

❏Name: _____ Phone: _____ Gifts   Thank You
Children:_____ Shower: _____ ❏
Address:_____ Shower: _____ ❏
City: _____ State: _____ Zip: _____ Wedding:_____ ❏
Wedding Invitation: ❏ Reception Invitation: ❏ Announcements: ❏ RSVP: Yes ❏ No ❏ Number Invited _____ Number Attending _____
❏Name: _____ Phone: _____ Gifts   Thank You
Children:_____ Shower: _____ ❏
Address:_____ Shower: _____ ❏
City: _____ State: _____ Zip: _____ Wedding:_____ ❏
Wedding Invitation: ❏ Reception Invitation: ❏ Announcements: ❏ RSVP: Yes ❏ No ❏ Number Invited _____ Number Attending _____
❏Name: _____ Phone: _____ Gifts   Thank You
Children:_____ Shower: _____ ❏
Address:_____ Shower: _____ ❏
City: _____ State: _____ Zip: _____ Wedding:_____ ❏
Wedding Invitation: ❏ Reception Invitation: ❏ Announcements: ❏ RSVP: Yes ❏ No ❏ Number Invited _____ Number Attending _____
❏Name: _____ Phone: _____ Gifts   Thank You
Children:_____ Shower: _____ ❏
Address:_____ Shower: _____ ❏
City: _____ State: _____ Zip: _____ Wedding:_____ ❏
Wedding Invitation: ❏ Reception Invitation: ❏ Announcements: ❏ RSVP: Yes ❏ No ❏ Number Invited _____ Number Attending _____
❏Name: _____ Phone: _____ Gifts   Thank You
Children:_____ Shower: _____ ❏
Address:_____ Shower: _____ ❏
City: _____ State: _____ Zip: _____ Wedding:_____ ❏
Wedding Invitation: ❏ Reception Invitation: ❏ Announcements: ❏ RSVP: Yes ❏ No ❏ Number Invited _____ Number Attending _____
❏Name: _____ Phone: _____ Gifts   Thank You
Children:_____ Shower: _____ ❏
Address:_____ Shower: _____ ❏
City: _____ State: _____ Zip: _____ Wedding:_____ ❏
Wedding Invitation: ❏ Reception Invitation: ❏ Announcements: ❏ RSVP: Yes ❏ No ❏ Number Invited _____ Number Attending _____
❏Name: _____ Phone: _____ Gifts   Thank You
Children:_____ Shower: _____ ❏
Address:_____ Shower: _____ ❏
City: _____ State: _____ Zip: _____ Wedding:_____ ❏
Wedding Invitation: ❏ Reception Invitation: ❏ Announcements: ❏ RSVP: Yes ❏ No ❏ Number Invited _____ Number Attending _____
Name: _____ Phone: _____ Gifts   Thank You
Children:_____ Shower: _____ ❏
Address:_____ Shower: _____ ❏
City: _____ State: _____ Zip: _____ Wedding:_____ ❏
Wedding Invitation: ❏ Reception Invitation: ❏ Announcements: ❏ RSVP: Yes ❏ No ❏ Number Invited _____ Number Attending _____
❏Name: _____ Phone: _____ Gifts   Thank You
Children:_____ Shower: _____ ❏
Address:_____ Shower: _____ ❏
City: _____ State: _____ Zip: _____ Wedding:_____ ❏
Wedding Invitation: ❏ Reception Invitation: ❏ Announcements: ❏ RSVP: Yes ❏ No ❏ Number Invited _____ Number Attending _____
❏Name: _____ Phone: _____ Gifts   Thank You
Children:_____ Shower: _____ ❏
Address:_____ Shower: _____ ❏
City: _____ State: _____ Zip: _____ Wedding:_____ ❏
Wedding Invitation: ❏ Reception Invitation: ❏ Announcements: ❏ RSVP: Yes ❏ No ❏ Number Invited _____ Number Attending _____
❏Name: _____ Phone: _____ Gifts   Thank You
Children:_____ Shower: _____ ❏
Address:_____ Shower: _____ ❏
City: _____ State: _____ Zip: _____ Wedding:_____ ❏
Wedding Invitation: ❏ Reception Invitation: ❏ Announcements: ❏ RSVP: Yes ❏ No ❏ Number Invited _____ Number Attending _____

❑Name: _____ Phone: _____ Gifts   Thank You
Children:_____ Shower: _____ ❑
Address:_____ Shower: _____ ❑
City: _____ State: _____ Zip: _____ Wedding:_____ ❑
Wedding Invitation: ❑ Reception Invitation: ❑ Announcements: ❑ RSVP: Yes ❑ No ❑ Number Invited _____ Number Attending _____

❑Name: _____ Phone: _____ Gifts   Thank You
Children:_____ Shower: _____ ❑
Address:_____ Shower: _____ ❑
City: _____ State: _____ Zip: _____ Wedding:_____ ❑
Wedding Invitation: ❑ Reception Invitation: ❑ Announcements: ❑ RSVP: Yes ❑ No ❑ Number Invited _____ Number Attending _____

❑Name: _____ Phone: _____ Gifts   Thank You
Children:_____ Shower: _____ ❑
Address:_____ Shower: _____ ❑
City: _____ State: _____ Zip: _____ Wedding:_____ ❑
Wedding Invitation: ❑ Reception Invitation· ❑ Announcements: ❑ RSVP: Yes ❑ No ❑ Number Invited _____ Number Attending _____

❑Name: _____ Phone: _____ Gifts   Thank You
Children:_____ Shower: _____ ❑
Address:_____ Shower: _____ ❑
City: _____ State: _____ Zip: _____ Wedding:_____ ❑
Wedding Invitation: ❑ Reception Invitation: ❑ Announcements: ❑ RSVP: Yes ❑ No ❑ Number Invited _____ Number Attending _____

❑Name: _____ Phone: _____ Gifts   Thank You
Children:_____ Shower: _____ ❑
Address:_____ Shower: _____ ❑
City: _____ State: _____ Zip: _____ Wedding:_____ ❑
Wedding Invitation: ❑ Reception Invitation: ❑ Announcements: ❑ RSVP: Yes ❑ No ❑ Number Invited _____ Number Attending _____

❑Name: _____ Phone: _____ Gifts   Thank You
Children:_____ Shower: _____ ❑
Address:_____ Shower: _____ ❑
City: _____ State: _____ Zip: _____ Wedding:_____ ❑
Wedding Invitation: ❑ Reception Invitation: ❑ Announcements: ❑ RSVP: Yes ❑ No ❑ Number Invited _____ Number Attending _____

❑Name: _____ Phone: _____ Gifts   Thank You
Children:_____ Shower: _____ ❑
Address:_____ Shower: _____ ❑
City: _____ State: _____ Zip: _____ Wedding:_____ ❑
Wedding Invitation: ❑ Reception Invitation: ❑ Announcements: ❑ RSVP: Yes ❑ No ❑ Number Invited _____ Number Attending _____

Name: _____ Phone: _____ Gifts   Thank You
Children:_____ Shower: _____ ❑
Address:_____ Shower: _____ ❑
City: _____ State: _____ Zip: _____ Wedding:_____ ❑
Wedding Invitation: ❑ Reception Invitation: ❑ Announcements: ❑ RSVP: Yes ❑ No ❑ Number Invited _____ Number Attending _____

❑Name: _____ Phone: _____ Gifts   Thank You
Children:_____ Shower: _____ ❑
Address:_____ Shower: _____ ❑
City: _____ State: _____ Zip: _____ Wedding:_____ ❑
Wedding Invitation: ❑ Reception Invitation: ❑ Announcements: ❑ RSVP: Yes ❑ No ❑ Number Invited _____ Number Attending _____

❑Name: _____ Phone: _____ Gifts   Thank You
Children:_____ Shower: _____ ❑
Address:_____ Shower: _____ ❑
City: _____ State: _____ Zip: _____ Wedding:_____ ❑
Wedding Invitation: ❑ Reception Invitation: ❑ Announcements: ❑ RSVP: Yes ❑ No ❑ Number Invited _____ Number Attending _____

❑Name: _____ Phone: _____ Gifts   Thank You
Children:_____ Shower: _____ ❑
Address:_____ Shower: _____ ❑
City: _____ State: _____ Zip: _____ Wedding:_____ ❑
Wedding Invitation: ❑ Reception Invitation: ❑ Announcements: ❑ RSVP: Yes ❑ No ❑ Number Invited _____ Number Attending _____

❑Name: _____ Phone: _____ Gifts   Thank You
Children:_____ Shower: _____ ❑
Address:_____ Shower: _____ ❑
City: _____ State: _____ Zip: _____ Wedding:_____ ❑
Wedding Invitation: ❑ Reception Invitation: ❑ Announcements: ❑ RSVP: Yes ❑ No ❑ Number Invited _____ Number Attending _____

❑Name: _____ Phone: _____ Gifts   Thank You
Children:_____ Shower: _____ ❑
Address:_____ Shower: _____ ❑
City: _____ State: _____ Zip: _____ Wedding:_____ ❑
Wedding Invitation: ❑ Reception Invitation: ❑ Announcements: ❑ RSVP: Yes ❑ No ❑ Number Invited _____ Number Attending _____

❑Name: _____ Phone: _____ Gifts   Thank You
Children:_____ Shower: _____ ❑
Address:_____ Shower: _____ ❑
City: _____ State: _____ Zip: _____ Wedding:_____ ❑
Wedding Invitation: ❑ Reception Invitation: ❑ Announcements: ❑ RSVP: Yes ❑ No ❑ Number Invited _____ Number Attending _____

❑Name: _____ Phone: _____ Gifts   Thank You
Children:_____ Shower: _____ ❑
Address:_____ Shower: _____ ❑
City: _____ State: _____ Zip: _____ Wedding:_____ ❑
Wedding Invitation: ❑ Reception Invitation: ❑ Announcements: ❑ RSVP: Yes ❑ No ❑ Number Invited _____ Number Attending _____

❑Name: _____ Phone: _____ Gifts   Thank You
Children:_____ Shower: _____ ❑
Address:_____ Shower: _____ ❑
City: _____ State: _____ Zip: _____ Wedding:_____ ❑
Wedding Invitation: ❑ Reception Invitation: ❑ Announcements: ❑ RSVP: Yes ❑ No ❑ Number Invited _____ Number Attending _____

❑Name: _____ Phone: _____ Gifts   Thank You
Children:_____ Shower: _____ ❑
Address:_____ Shower: _____ ❑
City: _____ State: _____ Zip: _____ Wedding:_____ ❑
Wedding Invitation: ❑ Reception Invitation: ❑ Announcements: ❑ RSVP: Yes ❑ No ❑ Number Invited _____ Number Attending _____

❑Name: _____ Phone: _____ Gifts   Thank You
Children:_____ Shower: _____ ❑
Address:_____ Shower: _____ ❑
City: _____ State: _____ Zip: _____ Wedding:_____ ❑
Wedding Invitation: ❑ Reception Invitation: ❑ Announcements: ❑ RSVP: Yes ❑ No ❑ Number Invited _____ Number Attending _____

Name: _____ Phone: _____ Gifts   Thank You
Children:_____ Shower: _____ ❑
Address:_____ Shower: _____ ❑
City: _____ State: _____ Zip: _____ Wedding:_____ ❑
Wedding Invitation: ❑ Reception Invitation: ❑ Announcements: ❑ RSVP: Yes ❑ No ❑ Number Invited _____ Number Attending _____

❑Name: _____ Phone: _____ Gifts   Thank You
Children:_____ Shower: _____ ❑
Address:_____ Shower: _____ ❑
City: _____ State: _____ Zip: _____ Wedding:_____ ❑
Wedding Invitation: ❑ Reception Invitation: ❑ Announcements: ❑ RSVP: Yes ❑ No ❑ Number Invited _____ Number Attending _____

❑Name: _____ Phone: _____ Gifts   Thank You
Children:_____ Shower: _____ ❑
Address:_____ Shower: _____ ❑
City: _____ State: _____ Zip: _____ Wedding:_____ ❑
Wedding Invitation: ❑ Reception Invitation: ❑ Announcements: ❑ RSVP: Yes ❑ No ❑ Number Invited _____ Number Attending _____

❑Name: _____ Phone: _____ Gifts   Thank You
Children:_____ Shower: _____ ❑
Address:_____ Shower: _____ ❑
City: _____ State: _____ Zip: _____ Wedding:_____ ❑
Wedding Invitation: ❑ Reception Invitation: ❑ Announcements: ❑ RSVP: Yes ❑ No ❑ Number Invited _____ Number Attending _____

Quick Reference
Names and Phone Numbers

Family/Bridal Party

NAME

PHONE NUMBER

_____
_____
_____
_____
_____
_____
_____
_____
_____
_____
_____
_____
_____
_____
_____
_____
_____
_____
_____
_____
_____
_____

Ceremony/Reception Site

NAME

PHONE NUMBER

_____
_____
_____
_____
_____
_____

Professional Services

NAME   PHONE NUMBER

_____   _____
_____   _____
_____   _____
_____   _____
_____   _____
_____   _____
_____   _____
_____   _____
_____   _____

Party Hostesses

NAME   PHONE NUMBER

_____   _____
_____   _____
_____   _____
_____   _____

Others

NAME   PHONE NUMBER

_____   _____
_____   _____
_____   _____
_____   _____

Future Home

ADDRESS   PHONE NUMBER

_____   _____

OUR WEDDING KEEPSAKE

Something old _____

    given by _____

Something new _____

    given by _____

Something borrowed _____

    given by _____

Something blue _____

    given by _____

Bridal bouquet caught by _____

_____

Bride's garter caught by _____

_____

Special memories of the day _____

_____

_____

_____

_____

_____

_____

_____

_____

_____

_____

_____

_____

_____

_____